★ A PLACE FOR US ★

A PLACE FOR US

HOW TO MAKE SOCIETY CIVIL AND DEMOCRACY STRONG

BENJAMIN R. BARBER

HILL AND WANG

A DIVISION OF FARRAR, STRAUS AND GIROUX

NEW YORK

Hill and Wang
A division of Farrar, Straus and Giroux
19 Union Square West, New York 10003

Distributed in Canada by Douglas & McIntyre Ltd.
Printed in the United States of America
Designed by Abby Kagan
First edition, 1998

Library of Congress Cataloging-in-Publication Data
Barber, Benjamin R., 1939–
    A place for us: how to make society civil and democracy strong /
by Benjamin R. Barber. — 1st ed.
        p.   cm.
    Includes bibliographical references and index.
    ISBN 0-8090-7657-8 (alk. paper)
    1. Civil society.   2. Democracy.   I. Title.
JC336.B25   1998
301 — dc21   97-44914

FOR LEAH

who made "a place for us"
much more than the title of a book

CONTENTS

★ A PLACE FOR US ★

Our world, on the threshold of the millennium, grows crowded: too many people, too much anarchy, too many wars, too much dependency. Plagued by the effects of this crowding—conflict, alienation, the colonization of our everyday lives by bureaucracy and markets, the erosion of traditional work, a scarcity of meaningful jobs—we look, often in vain, for hospitable spaces to live in, for common ground where we can arbitrate our differences or survive them with civility, for places where we can govern ourselves in common without surrendering our plural natures to the singular addictions of commerce and consumerism. A place for us: that is all we seek. A place that allows full expression to the "you" and "me," the "we" of our commonalty, a place where that abstract "we" discloses the traces that lead back to you and me.

Walt Whitman followed the traces from the great American abstraction back to its palpably human constituency:

> *O I see flashing that this America is only you and me,*
> *Its power, weapons, testimony, are you and me,*

Its crimes, lies, thefts, defections, are you and me,
Its Congress is you and me, the officers, capitols, armies,
ships, are you and me. . . .
Natural and artificial are you and me,
Freedom, language, poems, employments are you and me,
Past, present, future, are you and me.

I dare not shirk any part of myself,
Not any part of America good or bad . . . [1]

In an ideal civic architecture of free nations, the space that accommodates the mutuality of "you and me" is civil society. The very phrase suggests an independent domain of free social life where neither governments nor private markets are sovereign; a realm we create for ourselves through associated common action in families, clans, churches, and communities; a "third sector" (the other two are the state and the market) that mediates between our specific individuality as economic producers and consumers and our abstract collectivity as members of a sovereign people. The philosopher Michael Walzer's spare language calls civil society "the space of uncoerced human association and also the set of relational networks—formed for the sake of family, faith, interest and ideology—that fill this space."[2] Trouble is, the relational networks of family and faith that fill the space of uncoerced association are themselves often coercive. This paradox is at the heart of the distinctions among types of civil society I will propose.

Like all political constructs, civil society is not singular in meaning or ideological intent. It has been many things and played many roles in many different epochs and places. In despotic communist and fascist states, it has been an imagined future land of liberty and as such has given dissidents and rebels a high-octane engine of revolt. In centralized states, it has been an imagined land of ancient municipal liberties and as such has given conservatives a blunt instrument with which to resist state activism. (Thus did Alexis de Tocqueville, in his *The Ancient Regime and the French Revolution*, appeal to the traditional freedom of France's once sovereign regional *parlements* when he surveyed the destruction wrought not only by the Revolution but by the centralizing tendencies of the Bourbon kings.) Liberals, too, have used civil society as a caution against government gargantuanism. When in his 1996 State of the Union address President Bill Clinton proclaimed the end of the era of big government, he gave a certain progressive legitimacy to a twenty-year-old conservative campaign against government in general. But being against government does not necessarily produce a program on behalf of civil society.

Among radical economic conservatives, the call to dismantle government has been accompanied by an appeal to markets. Though they are private, rapacious, and uncivil, markets have become for such conservatives a synonym for civil society. People are understandably impatient with metastasizing government bureaucracy, but when they succumb to the logic that proposes markets in its stead, they risk rationalizing a wholesale privatization that leaves those in need dependent on the uncertain mercies of the market and robs those who seek cooperative democratic solutions to their problems of the public instruments they need to discover and execute a common will. Big government has always been an ally of the little guy, and downsizing it has generally been a recipe for upgrading the power of private-sector monopolies. Schoolroom bullies are forever questioning the legitimacy of hallway monitors. The recent abolition in the United States of "welfare as we know it," conspired in by Democrats and Republicans alike, is a monument to an infectious fear of government that puts those most in need most at risk.

This book has as its premise a challenge both to self-abnegating politicians who use the ideal of civil society to campaign against politics and to laissez-faire critics who use it as a synonym for privatization and insist that the market can cure every social ill. My premise—my promise—is that only in the civic terrain lying between the extremes of "Prince and Merchant," of big government and wholly private commercial markets, can we mediate between public and private, between community and individual, and between the power of public communities and the liberty of private individuals. The idea of civil society can democratize our "princes" and thus relegitimize government at the same time that it civilizes and thus tames our merchants.

Civil society is not an alternative to democratic government but, rather, the free space in which democratic attitudes are cultivated and democratic behavior is conditioned. It is not a synonym for the private market but an antidote to commercial selfishness and market incivility. It treats democratic government as civil association's highest form of expression—the association of all associations: that is, common action in the name of liberty raised to its most general level. Civic renewal thus means democratic renewal. Tocqueville captured perfectly the relation between initially self-interested action and democratic citizenship when he waxed enthusiastic about young America's fondness for civic association:

> As soon as several of the inhabitants of the United States have taken up an opinion or a feeling which they wish to promote in the world, they look for mutual assistance, and as soon as they have found each other out, they combine. From that moment, they are no longer isolated men, but a power seen from afar. . . . thus, the example of civic cooperation can give citizens a sense of their interdependence and power. It trains people in the practice of citizenship.[3]

Civil society remedies the vices of dependency not with independence but with interdependence. It is the domain of you and me as we gather into active we's.

This is not to suggest that the idea of civil society is novel. Its currency today signals a renewed interest in an old idea, not fascination with social innovation. In just a few turbo-media years, civil society in the West has gone from being an esoteric preoccupation of intellectual historians concerned with the influence of Locke, Hegel, and Marx to being a chic catch phrase, as ideologically malleable as it is—for many of its less thoughtful fans— substantively vapid. People stirring it in with terms such as communitarianism, civic republicanism, trust, free markets, and civic virtue have thought they were cooking up a new menu of political choices. Those choices are not yet much in evidence, however, and one aim of this book is to make them both concrete and manifest. At the same time, people mulling over new recipes for civil society have offered political fare often tastier for its novelty than for its meaning. Citizens certainly have grounds to be attracted to and suspicious toward so elastic and novel and at times empty an idea.

The many American experiments associated with the new interest in civil society have, altogether appropriately, elicited both hope and cynicism. Few observers have been overtly hostile to "worthy" projects (who could call them unworthy?) like the privately funded National Commission on Civic Renewal, a bipartisan private effort co-chaired by William Bennett and Senator Sam Nunn, which in 1996–97 held hearings, commissioned essays, and produced a position paper;[4] or the Presidents' Summit on America's Future, a national conference on voluntarism chaired by General Colin Powell and inaugurated at a Volunteer Weekend in Philadelphia in April 1997, aimed at serving the needs of children; or the new and fashionable "civic journalism," a movement dedicated to encouraging the media to give us good news along with bad, inspiring anecdotes about local civic engagement along with the usual demoralizing tales of race crimes, kidnapping, child abuse, and murder. But still fewer independent observers would want to assert that such programs by themselves can be much more than bland cosmetic adornments on a sickly body politic. "Bipartisan" and "apolitical"—supposedly virtuous adjectives in the language of civil society—may suggest something laudable in an era as skeptical about politics as ours, but they also suggest tokenism and insipid efforts to avoid real problems. Ideological argument is an expression of the conflict of interests, and conflict is the raison d'être of politics. As Rousseau noted, if we were angels who lived in harmony, we would not need politics.

The truth is, conflict also infects the "neutral" pretensions of civil-society language. Just below the calm and would-be nonpartisan surface lies a struggle for the heart of civil society. After all, the idea has been championed by zealous partisans of almost every ideological persuasion: by European leftist dissidents opposing classical totalitarian government; by New Democrats in the neo-liberal center seeking alternatives to government that do not further corrupt political faith; by laissez-faire economic libertarians looking to embellish the idea of the free market with some social embroidery; and by Family Value Republicans on the reactive right, whose aim is to minimize the welfare state and replace it with a private republic of morals.⁵ In its susceptibility to such diverse usage, the idea of civil society is perhaps not so much nonpartisan as multipartisan. In a similarly ambiguous manner, it has also been used both by those who want to uncover the Lockean foundations of a liberal state as it might have manifested itself in the period of Tocqueville's visit to Andrew Jackson's America and by those who want to ground in some imagined future utopia their radical dissent and civic opposition to autocratic governments in eastern Europe or Latin America.⁶

The multipartisan character of the civil-society discussion has held out some promise of relief from the stale discourse of class warfare, to be sure. Ideological debate rooted in the class realities of nineteenth-century early industrial society is increasingly unsuited to the economic and social crises of a twenty-first-century post-industrial information society. But freed from any connection to ideology, the idea of civil society threatens to lose its purchase on politics, to blunt its edge by blurring conflicts of interest and softening questions of power, so that equality and social justice are left fuzzy or out of frame. A solution that promises salvation to every partisan may promise nothing in particular to anyone. Only a politics devoid of meaning can serve as a politics for everyman. I have said, politics is about differences. In distinguishing among several different ideological approaches to civil society, I hope not to abandon its core meaning but, in parsing the idea, to restore at least some of its political edge.

Discourse about civil society has gained leverage in recent years as a consequence of controversies over the supposed decline in social membership, social trust, and social capital in America, an issue that has been debated in the work of Robert Putnam, Francis Fukayama, Amitai Etzioni, Michael Sandel, William Bennett, Senator Dan Coats, Harry Boyte, and others.[7] The evidence is contested, but certain obvious trends are difficult to deny. Electoral participation in the United States scarcely reaches 50 percent today, even in Presidential elections, and is down by nearly thirty points from historical highs; meanwhile, membership in such symbolic civic groups as parent-teacher associations has fallen by nearly a half during the last thirty years.[8] If, as many have argued, membership in traditional forms of civil and voluntary associations is declining, if voter turnout is in free fall, and if social trust is in jeopardy, and if all this is in some fashion related to what we mean by civil society, the repair of civil society becomes a sine qua non of democratic survival.

President Clinton's promise to "repair the breach" is, precisely, about the promise of civil society—or it is about nothing at all. When leaders of societies in transition from autocratic to democratic governments use that same promise to justify resistance, they, too, make it the sine qua non of democratic development. But this depends on understanding clearly what civil society actually means, not only in the abstract but in its everyday practices — in all its many different contexts, past and present, American and European, revolutionary and conservative. We must inquire what it means not only as a description of social organization but as a prescription for how society might ideally be organized, how one might treat the ills of living democracy or catalyze democratization in societies not yet free.

In this book, then, I have just a few clear and closely linked purposes. My first objective is to offer a framework for conceptual clarification that creates order from the current chaos of usage. While this involves a degree of theoretical analysis that may try the patience of readers who are concerned more with political crisis than with political theory, I do not know how to proceed intelligently with effective democratic change that rests on the idea of civil society without first trying to make sense of the idea itself.

My second purpose is to tease out an interpretation of civil society that is persuasively progressive and democratic: broad and attractive to a variety of traditional partisans, but useful especially to those who are partisans of democratic struggle and social justice. I shall try, in other words, to justify a strong, democratic, and progressive interpretation of civil society, and if this leads back to more ideological kinds of argument, I shall not complain.

My third objective is to offer a series of concrete proposals and practical strategies aimed at reestablishing (or, where they already exist, reenforcing) institutions and practices at the heart of a strong democratic civil society. Globalizing markets and anti-governmental paranoia have obscured our civic vision, making it hard for us to see that there is a place for us between big government and commercial markets, where citizens can breathe freely and behave democratically without regarding themselves as passive complainers, grasping consumers, or isolated victims.

If I can achieve these three objectives, I may be able to place the reconceived idea of civil society in the context of two pressing current problems: the growing incivility of our public discourse (incivility betokens an uncivil society); and the "end of work," the problem of enforced "leisure" in democracies where wage labor has been the foundation of the value system but where society is becoming far better at producing goods than at producing jobs. These two issues exemplify, as well as almost any, the vital relationship between a robust civil society and a healthy democracy.

1

THREE KINDS OF CIVIL SOCIETY

So important has civil society become to the conduct of politics today that nearly everyone has his own notion of what it means. Is there a core conception or objective definition we can agree on? Do not count on social science for an answer. I do not share the naïve view that facts and values can be easily sorted out and kept in splendid isolation (a point of view that social scientists call "positivism"). Rather, I believe that politics demarcates a zone that conflates the actual and the ideal. Therefore, as a political phrase, civil society has both empirical and normative meanings. It tells us something about how we actually do behave even as it suggests an ideal of how we ought to behave. Efforts to extricate our ideals from our actual practices usually end by nullifying the meaning of both. Academic political science has all too often been guilty of exactly this kind of nullification. As the historian Alfred Cobban remarked, what passes as empirical "political science" is frequently a device for avoiding politics without achieving science.

Civil society describes both certain kinds of institution and social membership (a social scientist would say it can be captured by certain empirical indicators and be made the subject of observation and comparison, as well as prediction and experiment); and certain of our ideals (social scientists would say that in doing so it is normative rather than empirical, referring to our values and purposes). My claim is that when we use an inescapably political term like civil society, its ideal normative meaning as given by certain democratic and civic ideals is inextricably bound up with various civic attitudes and practices that surround it in our lives. What we understand as politics is tied to what we want from politics. The interdependence of the ideal and the actual does not mean that "anything goes," but it does close the door on some simplistic notion that we can easily arrive at an "objective" definition, or that there are "scientific" answers to our political questions.

I shall also avoid, in what follows, a genealogical account of civil society, though it has a long and noble history as a primary construct in Western political philosophy at least since the Enlightenment. John Locke as well as Scottish Enlightenment philosophers such as the two Adams, Smith and Ferguson, contributed to its early popularity as a notion of what linked the state and the individual, just as Hegel and Marx gave it a radical turn that allowed it to become both a reflection and a critique of bourgeois society. Tocqueville helped to introduce the idea into American political discourse, where it has exercised an important if somewhat paradoxical influence ever since. Indeed, few political speeches can come to an end nowadays without a reference to Tocqueville and his affection for civil society and its local institutions. (I did not manage to introduce this essay without dragging in his good name several times.) But this lively history no more determines or limits the ideal of civil society in political discussion today than Smith's eighteenth-century account of laissez-faire liberalism determines or limits modern debates about global market economics. We all depend on intellectual history, but this does mean we must constantly engage in it.[1]

Still, we are obliged to observe responsibly the distinctions that inhere in the diverse political circumstances of our own era. In recent decades, the notion of civil society has flourished in two very distinct political environments and continues to be pertinent in both. In eastern Europe and other once dictatorial societies in Latin America and Asia, it became a way of talking about samizdat politics and dissent, of alluding as much to what was absent in autocracy as to anything present in the critics' and dissenters' paltry institutions. In this kind of context, it has had a radical utopian cast: the imagined civil society we would ideally like to have, used as a critique of the despotic regimes we actually do have. It has also been a map for democrats discovering, as many recently have, that to democratize a state and liberalize an economy is not necessarily to establish a domain of real democratic freedom, unless, at the same time, society is civilized and pluralized through the cultivation of educational, philanthropic, religious, and other forms of civic association.

In well-established democracies, on the other hand, the idea of civil society has often been used to point back to foundational ideals which, although in crisis today, have a history and an institutional legitimacy. In this setting, civil society has been an appeal to what we once had used as a reproach to what now is.

The first usage, so popular in eastern Europe in the 1980s, appeals to an ideal pure and simple, and to a program for establishing new institutions. It is therefore almost always a feature of radical and utopian strategies.[2] The second usage, in the United States and western Europe today, appeals to a sociological heritage, to a program for reviving old institutions. It is therefore, even when used by liberal democrats, a feature of nostalgic if not quite conservative or even reactionary strategies, looking back to earlier ideals in order to reform current practices. The richness of face-to-face life in village England, of free communes in Switzerland, of the *mir* in old Russia, suggests the communitarian potential that certain historical civil society constructions might have today. This is why communitarian appeals to civil society may at one and the same time seem to offer a radical critique of current practices *and* to call up a conservative ideology rooted in family values and traditional mediating institutions.

The appeal to civil society, then, even in its radical incarnation, often manifests itself as an appeal to the past, to memory. The Polish intellectual Stansislaw Baranczak writes of artists in repressive regimes: "In Eastern and Central Europe any action of antitotalitarian resistance was always identified with saving or reviving 'memory.' We were in the business of rectifying distortions. They [official apparatchik artists] were appointed, or just hired, by the regimes to help invalidate memory; we were appointed by no one other than ourselves to help invalidate the invalidation."[3]

For the most part, I am concerned here with established democracies like those of the United States and western Europe, and I shall try to fix usage in the context of civil society as it is understood as an existing legacy from our own democratic pasts. Its advocates are often inclined to say that civil society must be retrieved from some imagined (not to say imaginary) now vanished earlier world—of France's medieval *parlements*, for example, or Switzerland's ancient confederalism, or Italy's and Holland's free city-republics. As I shall suggest, democratizing or even radical uses for civil society occur even where the ideal is drawn from imagined history.

We can isolate and illuminate three distinct views on civil society found within this "foundationalist" heritage that affects to retrieve and use ancient root ideals: what I will call the libertarian, the communitarian, and the strong democratic models. These three versions of the idea of civil society share and rest upon an even more traditional distinction between the state and the individual, between the public and the private sectors. This makes for a rather complicated picture, the equivalent in music of counting out three beats against a two-beat phrase. My three beats are the three domains of state, civil society, and market (or politics, society, and economy), but I shall count them out against the two beats of public and private: the traditional polarized setting that treats state and individual, power and liberty, as adversaries. Of the three versions of civil society, the first two tend to mirror the simple dichotomy of public and private, of power and liberty; that is to say, civil society is thought of as a largely *private* domain, in distinction to the public domain of the state, a private domain defined by individuals and their corporations and communities. By assuming that civil society is simply a way of talking about the private, and leaving aside its public features, neither the libertarian nor the communitarian model serves as effectively as it might to make the revitalizing of civil society a condition for taming markets, civilizing society, and democratizing government.

THE LIBERTARIAN PERSPECTIVE: CIVIL SOCIETY AS A SYNONYM FOR THE PRIVATE SECTOR

It is easy enough to imagine that our lives and our institutions have only two possible venues, one public, the other private. The public one in this popular view is the domain of politics and universality, where we vote, pay taxes, fight wars, do jury service, discharge civic obligations, and claim services based on an idea of justice. The private one becomes the place where just about everything else occurs: where we work and play and pray and sleep and learn and produce and consume and reproduce.

This way of conceiving our political and our private lives as radical opposites suggests these two sectors of our living world are rival and largely incompatible. The first is the domain of the state and its formal governing institutions that we consider cynically as "it"; the second, a more sympathetic domain we think of as "us" that encompasses almost everything else we can imagine: from individuals to social organizations, from economic corporations to civil associations. The public sector is defined here by its power: the state *is* coercion, defined when it is a democratic state by its legitimate monopoly over force. The private sector is defined by liberty: the market *is* freedom, defined by voluntary contract and free association, and as such is the condition of privacy and individuality. This insistence on a bipolar interpretation is rooted in the illusory conviction that to be truly free we have to make a radical choice between government and markets.

In this most commonplace of all understandings, civil society is a synonym for the private market sector, a domain of free individuals who associate voluntarily in various economic and social groupings that are contractual in nature, including the family (which becomes a mini-corporation, a product of implicit contracts). With the state and the individual thus polarized, any growth in the one must come at the cost of attrition in the other. The two realms confront each other in a zero-sum game where any change in one entails an equal and opposite change in the other. More power, less liberty; more private, less public; and vice versa. When Senator Robert Dole offered Americans the choice of "trusting government or trusting the people," he polarized the public and private realms in just this way, leaving us only with the demonized "it" of public-sector government and the glorified multitudinous "me's" of the private-sector "we" he called "the people."

This classical libertarian model—setting the people and their government at odds and making power the nemesis of liberty and the state the enemy of the individuals it is supposed to serve—leaves no other venue for civil society but the private sector.* No

---

*There is considerable confusion nowadays about the term "liberalism." As used in modern ideological quarrels, "the 'L' word" is a synonym for leftist or progressive or welfare-statist programs and is used by conservatives to castigate "liberal

large distinctions can be made between individuals and the private civil associations they may form, between economic corporations and civil organizations, or between the realm of markets and the realm of culture, ethics, or religion (to take some emblematic instances). Dualism here creates an implacable (and improbable) opposition, which leaves those who are frustrated with government thinking that privatization is their only option. On the one hand, if we do not like government, we must downsize and limit it, privatize its civil functions, and leave individuals and their corporations and communities alone to do as they please. On the other hand, if you do not like your chances in the private market, turn to big government as your ally and guarantor. This offers us John Locke's choice between the anarchy of a world run by "pole-cats and foxes" (a privatized civil society) or one where the foxes and pole-cats are tamed by a "sovereign lion" (the state) that is itself, however, a potentially deadly predator.

In the libertarian model, social relations both within the private sector and between it and the state sector feel like contract relations: a series of deals that free individuals or associations make in the name of their interests and goods and in defense of their liberties. The libertarian model hence is a version of the social-contract model: it has the "thin" feel of liberal social relations where the human nexus is severely attenuated; where, in the language of the philosopher Robert Nozick, people "live separate existences" among which "no moral balancing is possible" and where

---

tax and spend" big-government types. But in earlier times "liberal" referred to those who upheld the liberal or private sector against government or statist intervention, and in this usage it more aptly describes conservatives with a libertarian, anti-governmental bias, such as the modern Republican Party and the British Conservative Party. To avoid such complications, I will generally use the term "libertarian" when referring to classical "liberal" strategies of containing government to secure the private realm of liberty, and use "liberal" in its modern connotation as "progressive."

their "voluntary consent" is required every time one forges a relationship with another—whether in a business, a church, or a marriage.[4]

When the individual looks at government from the privileged sanctuary of the private sector, as she would in the libertarian model, she sees only a fearsome leviathan sometimes capable of serving her interests as a client of government bureaucracies or as a consumer of government services, but just as likely to swallow up her liberties whole. European survivors of fascist and communist despotism have good reason to worry about what government can do to liberty. The "politics of fear" typical of so many refugees from the war years who witnessed or experienced the cruelty of which unlimited government is capable—Karl Popper or Judith Shklar or Isaiah Berlin, to name three—are understandably suspicious of all state power.[5] To suggest to Catalans living in a Spain just emerging from the shadow of Franco's fascist rule, where civics meant perverse propaganda, that they could and should encourage a government-sponsored citizen education program is obviously to meet with distrust, though decades have passed since Franco's demise. Even the term "citizenship" may elicit unhappy memories of "Comrade Beria" and "Citizen Commissar" in Budapest or Moscow. But such fear is harder to comprehend in the United States, where the governing majority has forever been a "puppy dog tethered to a lion's leash," in Louis Hartz's poignant phrase in his *The Liberal Tradition in America*. We can understand why, at the time of the Founding, Americans as distrustful of democratic as of monarchical power secured a constitution that did as much to limit as to enable government. Yet today many Americans persist in their distrust, as if they were still English Whigs suspicious of George III's ambitions or refugees from Napoleonic *étatisme*. "A government powerful enough to give us all we want," President Ford was still proclaiming at the 1996 Republican Convention, "is powerful enough to take from us all we have." The prudent libertarian concludes that liberties must therefore be surrounded by a thick wall of rights.

Philosophers looking at the fretful citizen pursuing his economic interests and deploying defensive parapets of rights to defend himself against an encroaching state may come to regard him as little more than an economic animal: *homo economicus*, the citizen defined as a consumer of government services, not as a participant but only as a watchdog to the political representatives accountable to him. From the point of view of the citizen who sees himself as an economic animal, civil associations feel, at best, rather like consumer cooperatives or rights alliances. They permit people to protect themselves more efficiently and serve themselves more securely but have little to do with participation, cooperation, or sociability per se, let alone solidarity, community, or the pursuit of a commonweal such a community makes possible.

For people in our day who fear politics and trust only private power, markets are the ticket to freedom — and they come to consider them as an appropriate surrogate for civil society. In eastern Europe after the fall of communism, securing a civil society was often regarded as more or less the same thing as securing a free market: "Civil society can only go hand in hand with a free market economy," wrote the Russian journalist Sergei Grigoriev, to which the Hungarian editor Gyorgy Varga added, "It is the individual entrepreneur . . . who will lead in the establishment of voluntary associations, philanthropy and the other patterns of civil society."[6] To Western entrepreneurs, the free-market economy may even take precedence over a democratic civil society. Asked in the spring of 1996 to consider the impact of a possible collapse of democracy in Russia, Pepsi-Cola's director of east European relations allowed as how "we think we can survive and prosper whatever regime is going to be here," since, whatever happens, the Russians will not "turn back the clock on consumers and deny them modern, Western brands."

Civil society understood in this way as a surrogate for the private sector and a synonym for consumer choice presents freedom in a strong but wholly privatized sense and sociability in its very thinnest sense. This helps to explain why the strategies of privatization being used in the name of democratization in eastern Europe have yielded results that so frequently fail to sustain the civic culture on which democracy depends. Consumers enjoy newly acquired economic power and a novel sense of their rights, but they do not wear the textured mantle of engaged citizens and are ambivalent democrats at best. Thanks to democratic laws and democratized formal governmental institutions, these consumers become voters, but such voters do not become citizens in a deeper sense and democracy remains thin and unpersuasive. With shopping and voting deemed interchangeable activities, countries where shopping flourishes get mislabeled as electoral democracies. "Voting your dollars" (or your yen or your D-marks), an entirely private act that does not and cannot create public policy or common goods, is confused with voting *tout court*, and the shopping mall, a place for me, gets confounded with democracy, a place for us.

By focusing on the consumer who is burrowed into a shell of rights and thus — autonomous, solitary, and egoistic — likely to venture into the social sector only to get something from a service-station state whose compass of activities must be kept minimal, the libertarian model of civil society can envision only a rudimentary form of social relations that remains shallowly instrumental: the citizen as client, the voter as customer, the democratic participant as consumer. Rights are the only political weapon that such private citizens can imagine: claims on government, which, however, impose no corresponding obligations on them as citizens.

By the same token, the libertarian model treats liberty as hyperindividualistic. That is to say, it regards freedom as negative and reactive with a vengeance — oppositional to government and likely to survive only where politics and society are marginal and minimal. Liberty is reduced to the private choices that consumers make among goods from a menu they do not write. The libertarian model of civil society cannot soften relations between individual and state or mediate between them, as many of sociology's traditional systems have tried to do. Nineteenth-century sociologists like Ferdinand Toennies wrote of both society (*Gesellschaft*) and community (*Gemeinschaft*) as mediators of individuality in the setting of coercive states. The thinness of the libertarian version of civil society means that it is unresponsive to the yearning for community and solidarity which modern peoples living in mobile, post-industrial societies feel so deeply. (This is what Robert Bellah and his colleagues wrote about so movingly in their *Habits of the Heart*.) And it accounts for much of the communitarian frustration that attends thin liberal conceptions of civil society, a form of frustration that can be dangerous to democracy. For it is a basic law of modern politics that where democratic communities cannot be found to do the work of solidarity and identity which human existence seems to require, undemocratic communities that do so will appear. In the absence of alternatives, these undemocratic bands may well seem irresistible: where neighborhood associations are absent, gangs may appear; where spiritual communities go missing, makeshift sects will spring up; where political clubs wither, totalitarian movements can flourish.

THE COMMUNITARIAN PERSPECTIVE: CIVIL SOCIETY AS A SYNONYM FOR COMMUNITY

The communitarian idea of civil society responds to these frustrations, but often without giving up the presumption that the social world is sharply divided into just two domains, one governmental, the other private. Still, communitarians do not believe that the private domain is simply one of solitary, rights-bearing individuals, or hungry consumers, or grasping entrepreneurs. Rather, since they assume that people are embedded in communities and tied to one another by bonds that precede and condition their individuality, they envisage civil society as a complex welter of ineluctably social relations that tie people together, first of all into families and kinship associations like clans, and then into clubs, neighborhoods, communities, congregations, and more extended social hierarchies. Libertarians think of civil society as a play space for private individuals and for the voluntary and contractual associations they choose to contract into, and treat it as little more than a condition for solitude. Communitarians, on the other hand, think of civil society as a zone where people interact and are embedded in communities, and they treat it as the condition for all social bonding.

Communitarians begin with the premise that most human associations are given ("ascriptive") rather than chosen ("voluntary"). We are born as Jews or Catholics no less than as males and females, as Persians or Thais no less than as Caucasians or Orientals. We play little part in fashioning the communities into which we are born, and these communities have purposes that seem natural rather than instrumental for the most part. And though even the most "natural" associations may have been voluntary at some ancient time (traditions and ancient communities are also socially constructed), these traditional membership communities have been sanctioned by time and tradition in a manner that utilitarian and contractual organizations can never be. Today's artifice may of course become tomorrow's entrenched community, just as today's innovative practice may become tomorrow's hoary tradition.

Yet even if our highest hopes are but "contingent products" of a self-invented identity (as the skepticist liberal philosopher Richard Rorty has written),[7] the distinction between the ancient communities that we call "natural" and the new associations that seem so obviously "artificial" is palpable and politically consequential. Rorty does not seem to notice that just because today's natural communities were once artificially constructed does not diminish their conservative political potency as "ancient" and "natural" associations impregnable to today's fashions and popular whims. The Russell, Kansas, or Hope, Arkansas, to which a modern politician appeals as an ancient habitat for the molding of political character, and which looks "natural" compared to the contrived metropolises of urban industrial civilization, was itself once founded and contrived. But how different Hope and Russell still are from, say, Celebration, Disney's Florida newtown. This is the great lesson of Edmund Burke's account of England's "prescriptive constitution," an ancient artifice that for Burke gave the nation its modern common-law constitution, with its natural resistance to the whims of transient majorities.

If the defining actor of civil society in the libertarian model is, in the founding phase, the rights-bearing rebel, and in established democracies the rights-bearing consumer, in the communitarian model he is the clansman: the bondsman tied to community by birth, blood, and bathos. Citizenship here takes on a cultural feel and marks its territory by exclusion rather than inclusion, often specifying anonymous "others" and "outsiders" whose foreignness helps to define the excluding (thus exclusive) insiders' community.

The great virtue today of civil society comprehended in this way as a private, closed nexus of tightly knit communities is the social glue it offers to otherwise disparate individuals and groups in an ever more anarchic social and economic world. If the defining moment of modernity was the severing of social bonds ("All that is solid melts into air," wrote Marx) and the rationalization, secularization, and bureaucratization of social relations (Max Weber), then this communitarian solidarity and fraternity promise to give back membership to unanchored souls and to assuage the uncertainty and psychic isolation that attend their lives in post-traditional society. Solidarity may of course bring with it hierarchy, exclusivity, and conformity: citizens who identify their social membership with the particularism of one *Gemeinschaft* may not make very effective democrats. Indeed, in the absence of offsetting or mediating values not generated by communitarianism itself, the illiberal norms of authoritarianism, parochialism, inequality, paternalism, and hierarchy may be inevitable, as Alan Ehrenhalt has argued in his nostalgic study of Chicago in the 1950s called *The Lost City*, where he insists community entails authority and is eroded by choice. "Apart from the family," writes Pope John Paul II, "intermediate social groups play a primary role . . . preventing the fall of the masses into impersonality and anonymity—a too frequent occurrence in modern society."[8] Yet can such groups do the job Pope John Paul II wants them to do and remain open and democratic? Is a thicker community always less egalitarian, less open, less free?

There can of course be democratic communities, and a modern document like the communitarian leader Amitai Etzioni's Communitarian Platform certainly aspires to a more democratic form of communitarianism; the progressive Jewish editor of *Tikkun*, Michael Lerner, has promulgated a "Politics of Meaning" that tries to offer a just, egalitarian form of Jewish communitarianism.[9] Democracy is, however, neither a necessary nor even a probable attribute of communitarianism per se, and communitarians must constantly work at it and for it. Furthermore, as they apply standards of justice, equality, and inclusiveness to a social form of intimacy that resists such standards, they risk weakening their communitarian bonds. The paradox of community is that its solidarity is attenuated by the very pluralism and independence that make it possible. Democratic community is certainly no oxymoron, but community has ideal attributes that resist democracy, while democracy makes demands that can undermine community. Hierarchy is hardly community's preferred form, but it can reinforce many of the virtues community brings with it. Defined by an Other, or even by an Enemy, community finds a solidarity it may not be able to sustain if it is open and inclusive. We of course want it both ways: Solidarity *and* Freedom, thick community *and* inclusion. But in establishing civil society, we may have to choose.

Anglo-American liberalism has, classically, considered civil associations as little more than variations on the contractualist market corporation, but European communitarianism has tended to interpret economic corporations as little more than variations on the natural community—which may remind us of the organic corporatism imagined by Italian fascist thinkers such as Rocco and Gentile. The political danger of unvarnished communitarianism is that it tends to absorb, assimilate, and finally monopolize all public space. When America's "cultural conservatives" make war on consumer capitalism (Hollywood, for example) and on the thin, relativistic liberal state (Patrick Buchanan's culture wars), they are reviving deadly old notions of *Kulturkampf* and are using a colonialist cultural paradigm that assimilates both the state and the private sector. Classical liberalism, with its fear of politics, may insist on a high wall between the state and the private sector as well as on a minimalist governing apparatus, but it has little interest in governance per se except to limit its jurisdiction. It may envision free markets as apt surrogates for many functions of government, but its aim is to do away with government rather than to take it over.

Communitarians, on the other hand, seem sometimes to want to subordinate the state and its institutions to a larger community. When the Baptists declare war on Disney, they do more than challenge the corporation's "pro-gay" social policies and its trivialization of religion; they also make a case for a society-wide application of their moral norms. What is theocracy but the sovereignty of a religious community over the rest of society—over the state and economy too? Civil society is here the community of all communities, organic and whole, the source of all moral and political authority, including governmental authority. Where libertarians worry that state bureaucrats might impose substantive values on free individuals and groups, communitarians fear that the state may be corrosively agnostic and have no guiding values at all. They may seek cultural safety not in laissez-faire insulation from the state but in its cultural takeover — as Patrick Buchanan and Ralph Reed attempted in their 1992 and 1996 Presidential campaign efforts and as European rightists like Jörg Haider (of Austria's Freedom Party) and Jean-Marie Le Pen (of France's National Front) have done in their campaigns against libertarian anti-statists and welfare-state socialists. Islamic fundamentalist communities likewise make war on the thin, materialist forms of civil society favored by partisans of the free market (a battle that I focused on in my book *Jihad vs. McWorld*).

The implicit political aspirations of communitarianism were evident in the German ideal of *Volksgemeinschaft*. This ideal not only captured the communitarian aspirations of the reaction to the wan liberal politics of the Weimar Republic of the 1920s but in time came to subordinate politics to communitarian parochialism, with altogether disastrous consequences for Germany and the world. Virulent nationalism in its German form was rooted in a communitarian conception of the German people (*Volk*) that brooked no alternative identities. To be a "citizen" of the Weimar Republic, to be a mere producer or consumer, even to be a Catholic or a Bavarian, was to have an identity far too "thin" for a full-blooded Aryan German eager to distinguish his "bloodline" from that of a Gypsy or a Jew. The cultural prejudices of German identity politics, though hardly democratic, were certainly communitarian, and anti-commercial to boot. The German experience reminds us that the siren call of community, though attuned to deep needs in the human spirit, can be answered in ways that violate both liberalism and democracy. Civil society construed as a blood community can be as totalizing as a one-party state or as consumption-obsessed global markets. Communitarians are not always alive enough to this darker side of the yearning for communal identity. The heart whose habits they would serve is not always rational, and its need for love sometimes seems to depend on its need to hate.

Jörg Haider, of Austria's foreigner-baiting Freedom party, has worked hard to sanitize his image since his visit to the United States in 1996, and his new book is full of "new democratic" platitudes borrowed from Tony Blair and Bill Clinton that downplay his Austrian nationalist zeal. This remade communitarian who once had kind things to say about the S.S. but now likes to be photographed in front of an American flag and compared to Martin Luther (and even Martin Luther King) cannot, however, hide his deeply undemocratic communitarian disdain for politics and politicians or whitewash his belief that civil society must be anchored in "moral fundamentals" that trump both state and private sectors.[10]

American communitarians are pragmatic democrats for the most part, of course, and they operate in the safety of a "thin" but well-entrenched, hyper-liberal regime which probably benefits from their alternative "thick" perspective. For these reasons, as well as because of the acultural borrowing by cultural conservatives like Haider, we need to put generalizations about civil society in a historical and cultural context, to fit the recipe to a particular nation's conditions: in etatist France we ask for a more individualist perspective on mediating institutions; in Austria we judge communitarian claims against the backdrop of the nation's Nazi experiences; while in a radically individualized United States we appeal for a more communitarian perspective. Whether communitarians have few contextual constraints (Austria?) or many (the United States), the time may come when a tradition of individualism is not enough to insulate the zealous among them from virulent nativism. It certainly did not do so a century or more ago, when Know-Nothings, Protestant zealots, and other nativists launched noxious anti-immigration campaigns all across America.

Ironically, while both communitarian and libertarian versions of civil association polarize state and individual (or state and community) in the name of the wall between public and private, they tend in both cases to colonize the "other side." People who think of themselves primarily or exclusively as economic beings — consumers and producers — start thinking about government exclusively as a servicer of client needs; people who think of themselves primarily or exclusively in terms of their ethnic or tribal identity start thinking about government as a repository for their identity. In effect, they colonize public space with their private identities. When market liberals do this, they downsize the state until it nearly vanishes ("the best government is no government at all"), making the private sphere quite nearly sovereign — a totalizing presence in the face of which every identity other than that of the producer and consumer vanish; when communitarians do it, they subordinate the state to a larger community which the state must faithfully serve — whether that community is the fatherland, a *Volksgemeinschaft*, or some blood clan writ large (the "Austrian People," the "Scottish nation," the "Bosnian Serb state," or "Christian America"). Islam's aspirations to theocracy are a logical extension of communitarianism's totalizing tendencies.

Communitarians in the throes of a totalitarian temptation must also confront the paradox that the natural communities which they aspire to fortify are often in practice realized only artificially. Under modern conditions, where the environment for natural community has been undermined by secularism, by utilitarianism, and by the erosion of "natural" social ties, many communities claiming traditional or natural identities must make strenuously artificial efforts to reconstitute themselves as the organic natural communities they no longer are or can be. Their labors result in contrived "voluntary" associations pretending to be "natural communities." The Ku Klux Klan is no more a "clan" in the sense of an extended kinship association or a blood band than self-consciously hyphenated American identity groups such as Polish-Americans or African-Americans are really Polish or African. American-born Polish- and African-Americans may identify with remembered or reinvented cultural roots, but they quickly discern, when they visit their ethnic homelands, how remote those hypothetical identities are from the largely deracinated Americans they have inevitably become. Keith B. Richburg makes this point with disconcerting candor in his *Out of America: A Black Man Confronts Africa.*

Roots call on memory. But the "memory" appealed to by poets and patriots resisting tyranny can be a tricky faculty for a people liberated from dictatorship and trying to forge a common identity. Ebonics has only the most tenuous relationship to historical African languages like Swahili, but it serves African-American political purposes by drawing attention to how black street dialect complicates national "literacy" standards in the United States. Reconstituting a remembered but historically eroded identity is simply not the same as fashioning a community in anything like its original form. Indeed, many of the pathologies of modern communitarianism arise out of features not of real community but of an imitation that, because it only mimics its ideal, is thin and defensive despite its quest for thick and self-sufficient identity. Today's Islamic Jihad is defined as much by its modern enemies as by its Islamic theological essence, just as American Protestant fundamentalism today is more reactive to the secular, materialist culture around it than proactive on the model of early Augustinean Christianity or the Puritans' City on the Hill. The pathologies I explored under the rubric of "Jihad" in my book *Jihad vs. McWorld* are problems not so much of, say, a pre-colonial Ibo tribesman two centuries ago as they are of a cosmopolitan of Ibo origins living among members of other tribes in a commercial, post-colonial city like Lagos.

It may even be that the "new" iterations of old vanished communities are more troublesome than the originals. It was not the Alemanni or the Aryans but the Nazis who sought *Lebensraum* and made war in their name who afflicted our century so grievously. Historical "Serbia" and "Bosnia" visited far less tragedy on the world than their reinvented post-modern namesakes have done.

The imitations must try harder than the "natural" originals: the artificial ardor bred by their insecurity about roots makes them far more dangerous. That is why the new "democratic" Haiders and Le Pens may pose a greater threat to civility than the nationalist forebears from whom they so painstakingly pretend to distinguish themselves.

It is understandable that communitarians can be anxious in the face of cosmopolitan disorder and the spontaneous anarchy of radical individualism, for it is those aspects of modernity which, after all, they associate with the corruption of their earlier identities. No wonder that the face of traditional cultural communitarians is conservative, sometimes reactionary. The sociologist and cultural critic Richard Sennett once celebrated the urban (and urbane) uses of disorder that attend cosmpolitanism; although he later rued the "fall of public man," his fallen public man was a cosmopolitan, not a communitarian.[11] Communitarians are likely to fear creative anarchy and respond favorably to authoritative orderliness, and their fears will obviously serve neither liberty nor public man. The brilliant, conservative sociologist Robert Nisbet, for example, believed that the dimming of community in late Western civilization brought with it a devastating twilight of authority (the title of one of his later books). Many observers, including sociologists such as Peter Berger and Alan Ehrenhalt and political critics such as William Bennett, have linked the crisis in values today with the vanishing of order and authority, and of the institutions of family and church that nurtured them.[12] The connections between communitarianism and authority (as well as hierarchy) are not fixed or determinative, but they are well established in practice. This to some degree puts the onus on communitarians to show us how they will deflect the natural tendency of solidarity and fraternalism to evolve into authoritarianism and hierarchy.

This is why, for some people—often the young, the adventuresome, the creative—communitarianism can feel cloistered and airless: the trap of a small town in which local hierarchies, rigid rules, and too much intimacy forge an inflexible culture of convention and gossip that drives them to flight. Neither Bill Clinton nor Bob Dole spent much time during their adult lives in the village communities they celebrated as definitive of their hopes for America. The creative friction between cosmopolitan cities and small towns is marked by this tension between self-creation and ascriptive (given) identity. The identity that a deracinated city dweller—long since uprooted from some faintly remembered village childhood—seeks as a home for his yearnings may, for those still enmeshed in village life, appear as nothing so much as a prison. Village life as portrayed in literature enjoys this twin reputation: depicted through the gentle memories of nostalgia writers like Dylan Thomas and Thorton Wilder, it is a remembered sanctuary from the world's dismal urbanity, a child's Christman in Wales long ago, the town that was "our town" as we wish it might have been; depicted by unsentimental realists such as Toni Morrison or Thomas Hardy, it is little more than a death trap[13]—not our town but their town, the town without pity and the town without tolerance.

Michael Oakeshott, perhaps England's leading conservative thinker in this century, captured the spirit of the cosmopolitan when he wrote of a mobilizing Renaissance world peopled by "younger sons making their own way in a world which had little place for them, of foot-loose adventurers who left the land to take to trade, of town-dwellers who had emancipated themselves from the communal ties of the countryside, of vagabond scholars."[14] Such adventurers strode out across the threshold of modernity into a yearling urban world that had little room for the clan fealty of the Middle Ages. But in leaping from a stolid world of community into the frenzy of deracinated urban life, they prepared the ground for a later communitarian nostalgia. The small towns they abandoned for urban liberation were reconstructed by their great-grandchildren as imagined sanctuaries from urbanity's plagues and used as political ammunition in the war against modernity.

These manifold portraits of community and cosmopolis may represent literary antipodes, but they are not really so contradictory as they appear. They capture two dimensions of communal identity that stand as virtue and vice to the same attributes. And they reflect the distance traveled from earlier intimate face-to-face communities to the elephantine urban civilizations which define modern life for most Westerners and which have raised up the new communitarians as champions of an imagined, mostly vanished way of life.[15] They also explain why the communitarian perspective on civil society is fraught and problematic as social policy. For communitarians want to restore the qualities of ancient communities whose disappearance was an inevitable consequence of the very modernizing (and post-modernizing) trends they decry and for which they prescribe community as the remedy. The world upon which they wish to refound a civil society is the world we have lost. They offer us the place we yearn for but can reach only if we retreat to ancestral identities no longer truly our own. If civil society depends upon restoring a world we have lost, it may be that there can be no civil society at all.

But civil society need not be an exercise in nostalgia. That is the welcome message of the strong democratic perspective.

THE STRONG DEMOCRATIC PERSPECTIVE: CIVIL SOCIETY AS THE DOMAIN BETWEEN GOVERNMENT AND MARKET

When the legendary labor leader Samuel Gompers was asked what labor really wanted, his answer yielded a clear portrait of civil society as a theater of democracy. "What do we want?" he declared, in words inscribed on his statue near the Alamo in San Antonio, Texas:

We want more schoolhouses and less jails,
More books and less guns,

More learning and less vice,
More leisure and less greed,
More justice and less revenge,
We want more opportunity to cultivate our better nature.

Learning, leisure, justice, and opportunity: a solemn recipe for a democratic civil society, where free institutions and sociability can rest comfortably on citizenship without being captured by over-weening government. A strong democratic conception of civil society differs from the versions we have discussed so far because it explicitly ties civil society to citizenship. It rejects the diametric opposition of public and private sectors and posits instead a mediating third realm for our actual world of social engagement—a normative ideal for citizens who want reinvigorated civic activity that is neither as thin and uninspiring as market liberalism nor as thick and glutinous as clannish community.

The tendency of both libertarians and communitarians to conflate private with civil space (whether in the form of markets or of communities) condemns us to stark political choices that are neither desirable nor realistic. Contract associations and kinship communities, like their clones and imitations, certainly represent forms of human engagement, but neither offers room for us to engage with neighbors, friends, citizens, and strangers who must of necessity live together. We gain a far more flexible frame for political and civic debate when we imagine social space as having at least three distinct sectors, and think of ourselves as having plural identities and multiple purposes rather than singular destinies defined exclusively by blood or by economics.

This strong democratic perspective on civil society distinguishes public and private realms—a state sector occupied by government and its sovereign institutions, and a private sector occupied by individuals and their contract associations in the "market"—and presumes a third domain mediating between them, sharing the virtues of each. This third, independent sector is defined by its civic communities—their plurality is its essence—which are membership associations that are open and egalitarian enough to permit voluntary participation.

There is a tension here between the ideal conditions for a voluntaristic civil society and the actual groups we may want to regard as essentially civic in nature. Hence, we may wish to draw democratic civil society's perimeters generously enough to encompass groups that fall short of the pure democratic, voluntaristic ideal. Churches, for example, are obvious candidates for membership in civil society, but strong "voluntarists" might insist that only congregations made up of those who are, say, baptized as adults or who convert can qualify, conditions that would exclude most congregations, however, and that we would want to soften. Similarly, we would certainly wish to have a definition broad enough to include a primarily African-American civic group such as the N.A.A.C.P., which serves the interests of its own racial community in the name of broader racial harmony, as long as its membership is open to everyone.

Still, the dominant characteristic of the civic domain is, by its nature, that it is an open, public realm (like the state sector) which, however, is voluntary and noncoercive (like the private sector). Its constituent member communities must therefore have some aspect of openness and inclusion, for although it is "private," it partakes of the egalitarian non-exclusivity of the democratic public sector; and although it is public, it is neither sovereign nor coercive, and partakes of the liberty and voluntariness of the private sector. By having both public and private virtues, it has a powerful, strong democratic aspect. Its communities are created by common activity as well as common history, in public as well as private work, and they achieve a degree of equality not because, one by one, they are equally egalitarian, but because they are plural. The civic domain is home to many diverse entities, and that many-ness is its defining democratic characteristic. One by one, individual communities and groups may look sectarian, exclusionary, inegalitarian, and involuntary, but in combination they weave a fabric that is textured by variety and difference. It is civil society as a whole that is free, because it is a voluntary sector in which women and men can choose their own forms of association. If the Black Muslims are too nationalist for your taste, try the N.A.A.C.P or the Democratic Party or the Baptist Church or the League of Women Voters or the Ripon Society for young Republicans. Not all of these groups afford the same degree of internal liberty, but civil society affords the liberty to choose among them; each particular community imposes a particular identity, but civil society allows particular identities to layer and cross-cut, blunting their sharp edges and endowing citizens with plural natures less vulnerable to domination by a single thick identity. Thick communities can coexist in the thinner atmosphere of a liberal civil society; this means the liberality of a strong democratic civil society is measured by the features of the society at large rather than of every individual community. Rather than worrying, as I have, about whether religious congregations meet the liberal standards of an open civil society, one can heed Adam Smith's counsel. As the author not only of *The Wealth of Nations* but of the liberal idea of civil society wrote two hundred years ago: "The interested and active zeal of religious teachers can be dangerous and troublesome only where there is, either but one sect tolerated in the society, or where the whole of a large society is divided into two or three great sects."[16] Pluralism is the condition of liberty in a strong democratic civil society. More is better.

Strong democratic civil society looks in many ways like what might be called "civic republicanism," in that it has democratic virtues, encourages the habits and practices of democratic ways of living, and is defined by both publicness and liberty, egalitarianism and voluntarism. It is a model for an ideal democratic civil society:

with citizens who are neither mere consumers of government services and rights-bearers against government intrusion, on the one hand, nor mere voters and passive watchdogs for whom representative governors are only vestigially accountable, on the other. Rather, its democratic citizens are active, responsible, engaged members of groups and communities that, while having different values and conflicting interests, are devoted to arbitrating those differences by exploring common ground, doing public work, and pursuing common relations. Social relations in a strong democratic civil society are thicker and more rewarding than those afforded by markets or by the economic interactions of production and consumption, yet they are less solidaristic and inhibiting than those of blood communities. To be someone's neighbor in a park clean-up project may not feel as rewarding as being someone's blood brother, but it feels far more rewarding than being an anonymous fellow shopper at some mall or a solitary voter at a polling station.

I now want to turn in some detail to the strong democratic model of a civil society of neighbors, associates, and cooperating strangers, for it not only captures the traditional Tocquevillean idea of a civic republican civil society as it was historically practiced in the United States but represents a powerful normative ideal. Without indulging in untoward nostalgia—Tocqueville's America tolerated slavery and excluded women, Native Americans, and many others from the franchise—we should bear it in mind when we address the civic defects of democracy in crisis today—both in nations where democracy is established and in those where women and men are still struggling to achieve it.

2

A PLACE FOR US:
STRONG DEMOCRATIC CIVIL SOCIETY

There should be a place for us in civil society, a place really for *us*, for what we share and who, in sharing, we become. That place must be democratic: both public *and* free (non-coercive, non-statist). The strong democratic perspective on civil society distinguishes our civic lives both from our private lives as individual producers and consumers and from our public lives as voters and rights-claimants. It also has certain historical and socio-logical roots in an earlier epoch that, paradoxically, was both less inclusive and, for the included, more democratic.

Once upon a time, there was a vital middling choice for Americans between the opposing poles of government and market, state and individual, contract association and community, and it was admired and imitated elsewhere in the world. This third option was an independent sector whose principal characteristic was in-terdependence among its members. Though badly eroded today, it held the key to our country's early democratic energy and civic activism. The political theorist Michael Sandel offers a fascinating account of this traditional "civic republican" perspective (a cousin of what I call the "strong democratic" perspective), in *Democracy's Discontent*, a book with a decidedly communitarian bias. Although republicanism was hardly a golden age in our history—after all, it coexisted with slavery and with many franchise inequalities—it did, Sandel believes, link liberty to "sharing in self-government," which was understood as "deliberating with fellow citizens about the common good and helping shape the destiny of the political community."[1]

Because it coexisted with slavery and with the limitation of suffrage to white males (in some states, to propertied white males), this civic republicanism of the United States before the Civil War cried out for a democratic liberal counter-ideal of a kind that eventually supported what I have called the libertarian model of civil society. Nonetheless, however restricted the franchise, for those who were citizens liberty was rich and rewarding because it was local and personal, because it grew out of affirmative civic activity in the neighborhood, and was not defined in opposition to an alien state or a completely distinct domain of commerce. A modest governmental sphere and an unassuming commercial sector were easily overshadowed in most American communities at that time by an extensive civil society anchored by strong (and patriarchal) families and tied together by school, town, church, and voluntary association, and the conformism—Tocqueville's tyranny of public opinion—they bred. The Federalist Constitution and later the Unionist Republican Party, however expansive they looked by the standards of eighteenth-century Whig liberals, who deeply distrusted *all* government, were—by today's benchmarks—true studies in civic humility: little more than a President plus a post office. Though opponents feared he might turn the Presidency into a camouflaged monarchy, George Washington in fact governed the new nation with an executive staff that numbered only in the dozens and held as his model the Roman republican Cincinnatus, who retired to his farm after discharging the obligations of civil leadership. Washington did the same, and was as much revered for his reticence as for his leadership. The Bill of Rights (notably, the Tenth Amendment) reinforced republicanism locally by leaving to the civic discretion of the "states and the people" all powers not expressly delegated to the central government. For the first sixty or seventy years of our nation's life, postal workers were by far the most numerous (and, miraculously, efficient) of our federal employees. Beyond the post office, few constitutionally sanctioned government activities required large numbers of federal or state public officials and bureaucrats. The municipalities and neighborhoods were the real theater for civic action in the United States right up until the Civil War.

In this simpler time, people thought of themselves as citizens and their groups as civil associations; together they comprised civil society. Only after the Civil War, when the questions of union and secession over which the war had been fought, and the challenges of reconstruction in which it issued, put new burdens on the state, did civil society lose ground to a newly energized federal government and the growing power of capitalist corporations with an appetite for expansion and a tendency to monopoly. Once these corporations were legitimized at law as "legal persons" and limited liability partnerships, they began to supplant voluntary associations as the primary actors in nongovernmental life. Market forces pressed in, encroaching on and sometimes crushing civil society as they radically expanded. The federal government responded on behalf of the public weal with an aggressive campaign of its own, not directly involving the public, but representing the civic good. In taking on the powers it needed to confront the corporations, it inadvertently took its own toll on civil society, encroaching on it from the other side.

Squeezed between these warring monopoly sectors of state and corporation, civil society lost its preeminent place in American life. At some time during the era marked by the Administrations of the two Roosevelts (1901–8 and 1933–45), civil society in its classical republican incarnation vanished and its civic denizens were compelled to find sanctuary under the tutelage of either big government (their protectors and social servants) or the private sector, where schools, churches, and foundations now began to take on corporate identities and seemed to be no more than special-interest groups formed for the specific purposes of their members, and where families were left more or less to fend for themselves (to which challenge they proved inadequate). Whether the ends pursued by civil associations were, say, market profitability or national moral consciousness was irrelevant, since by definition all private associations had private ends.

Paradoxically, groups organized in desperate defense of the public interest found themselves cast as mere exemplars of plundering private-interest associations pursuing one more private good. As Harry Boyte and Nancy Kari remind us in *Building America*, virtually all work once had the sense of public work and was understood to contribute to strong democratic life.[2] But that has changed. When the unions tried to break the stranglehold of the companies over corporate labor forces, they were labeled as another special-interest group no better or worse than those against whom they struck, and in time they came to act that way, losing their place in popular mythology as authentic representatives of working people. Now, though they are still concerned with distributive justice (fair compensation), full employment, and the dignity of work for all, people often think of them as private-sector counterparts of corporations, and they often behave that way.

More recently, civil-rights and environmental groups have undergone the same redefinition. Civil rights have been transmogrified by their critics into a special interest of minority groups for which most Americans are supposed to have little sympathy. Policies like affirmative action, which were once merely liberal efforts to address a specific historical reality, attempts to offer every American an equal playing field regardless of history or circumstances, came to be understood as the outgrowth of special-interest politics asking for special privileges for special groups. The government was accused of playing favorites among competing private groups, rather than upholding common civic rights in a sector that was neither governmental nor private. In the public setting of civil society, there is at least an argument worth making for affirmative action; in the private, commercial sector, it often seems to be no more than an effort to twist the market rules that presume the equality of all players to the advantage of a competing, otherwise "equal" interest group.

Groups interested in protecting the environment have undergone much the same distortion. While favoring what is in theory a genuinely civic republican (i.e., public!) agenda of, say, clean air for all ("all" including the polluters, who after all are citizens, too), environmental groups were robbed of the middle ground by their opponents' polarization of society into public and private sectors. Nowadays, rather than developing a discussion on behalf of the civic good, environmentalists often feel compelled to engage defensively in strident, unlistening polemics focused as much on their own moral self-righteousness as on the common good, or on, say, the rights of hikers and bird-watchers deployed as counterweights to the rights of snowmobilers and loggers. In the face of adversarial interest politics, the public good that might bring together loggers and bird-watchers in a community of concern about sustainable environments goes missing.

Under these conditions, the "public good" cannot and has not survived as a reasonable public ideal. "Public work" is depreciated and becomes what public servants do to service their "clients" (citizens), while "work" is what the rest of us do in the private sector to earn a living. The older civil society tradition, where common work is what citizens do in cooperating on projects that benefit the whole community, seems to have vanished. (Our barn-raisings, or what the Swiss called *Gemeinarbeit* when they cleared mountain pasture together or built avalanche guards to protect an entire village, are examples that lasted into the twentieth century.) But the idea of common work has little political resonance today. When Boyte and Kari eloquently urge the virtue of "public work" upon their fellow citizens, Americans may suspect they are referring to the public-works division of the local highway department and wonder what it can possibly have to do with them.

This melancholy history leaves us stranded in an era where citizens can find neither a place for their civic activity nor a voice for their civility. As Michael Sandel has suggested, the vestigial liberalism of our times "conceives persons as free and independent selves, unencumbered by moral or civic ties they have not chosen. This shift [to] the libertarian vision lacks the civic resources to sustain self-government [and] ill-equips it to address the sense of disempowerment that afflicts our public life."[3] What are our options? To be passively serviced (or passively exploited) by a massive, busybody, bureaucratic state, where the word "citizen" has no resonance and the only relevant civic act is voting (which less than half the eligible electorate engage in)? Or to join in the selfish, radical individualism of a private sector where the word "citizen" also has no meaning and the only relevant activity is consuming (which just about everybody engages in)? Or, finally, to lapse into some invented communitarian identity that pretends to an antiquity it achieves only by dogmatic self-assertion and exclusiveness? (Sandel himself does not always sort out republican from communitarian dimensions of engagement.) In sum, to be a passive, sometime voter and vote the public scoundrels out of public office, and/or to be a consumer or a tribesman exercising private rights on behalf of private or community interests — these are the only remaining obligations of the much diminished office of citizen. Of course, you can become an X-American, where the X part occludes the American part, and citizenship as an inclusive, principled civic identity is replaced by some invented nativist tribalism. (This is, in fact, a rabid version of the white Anglo-Saxon Protestant hegemony multiculturalists so dislike.)

Sandel celebrates (and rues) the vanishing of a form of civic republicanism akin to what I have called strong democratic civil society: one that posits a third domain for civic engagement which is neither governmental nor strictly private yet shares the virtues of both. It offers a space for public work, civic business, and other common activities that are focused neither on profit nor on a welfare bureaucracy's client services. It is also a communicative domain of civility, where political discourse is grounded in mutual respect and the search for common understanding even as it expresses differences and identity conflicts. It extols voluntarism but insists that voluntarism is the first step to citizenship, not just an exercise in private character building, philanthropy, or noblesse oblige. This is the missing space, a place truly for us.

Strong democratic civil society, like Tocqueville's civic republican civil society, shares with government a sense of publicity and a regard for the general good and the common weal, yet, unlike government, it makes no claims to exercise a monopoly on legitimate coercion. It partakes in that liberty which is the special virtue of the private sector, and yet it is not individualistic or anarchic. Rather, it is a voluntary and in this sense "private" realm devoted to public goods. In a civil society that is the true domain of church, family, and voluntary association, "belonging" is not a surrogate for freedom but its condition and training ground.[4] Civil society's middling terms can potentially mediate between the state and private sectors, and offer women and men a space for activity that is voluntary *and* public. When the government appropriates the term "public" exclusively for affairs of state, the real public (you and me) ceases to be able to think of itself as public (as an "us"), and politicians and bureaucrats become the only significant "public officials." Then politics is professionalized and citizenship is transformed into a private occupation. It is hardly surprising that under such circumstances people withdraw into themselves, grow angry at politicians and cynical about democracy, and fall easily to the seductions of narcissistic consumerism or exclusionary tribalism.

Without civil society, citizens are homeless: suspended between big bureaucratic governments which they no longer trust (Robert Putnam's grievance) and private markets they cannot depend on for moral and civic values (Michael Lerner's or Amitai Etzioni's complaint). They are without a place to express their commonalty. The "commons" vanishes, and where the public square once stood, there are only shopping malls and theme parks and not a single place that welcomes the "us" that we might hope to gather from all the private you's and me's.

A free nation depends for its liberties first of all neither on formal democratic governing institutions nor on free commercial markets but on a vibrant and pluralistic civil society. We have noted how Tocqueville celebrated the *local* character of American liberty and thought that democracy could be sustained only through vigorous municipal civic activity of the kind that typified Andrew Jackson's America. He would scarcely recognize the United States today, where our alternatives are restricted to government gargantuanism and either market greed or identitarian parochialism, and where the main consequence of recent elections seems to be that New Deal arrogance has been supplanted by market triumphalism. Both Speaker Newt Gingrich's Republicans and President Clinton's Democrats have proclaimed the end of the era of big government without identifying alternatives to the solitude and greed that are the private sector's facile triumphs.

The effect of these theoretical models on actual policy debates is evident in, say, the recent fiasco over whether and how to improve American health care. The Clinton Administration's plan for health-care reform failed in a paroxysm of mutual recrimination. But it was the policy process instigated by the Administration itself as much as the enemies of reform that brought the plan down. In what became an ever more technocratic and professionalized debate about what reform required in the abstract, the public at large simply went missing. Experts with public credentials debated experts with private credentials, but the people in whose names reforms were being drawn up were largely invisible. The merits of Oregon's health plan can be debated, but Oregon *got* a plan because it took care to have civic debates about it in specially created institutions like health parliaments which became central to the policy-making process. In the federal debate, the actual public was without a voice and those in search of it hardly knew where to look: neither opinion surveys nor the special-interest groups claiming to speak for the people (often in negative television ads) were representative of the American people. The abyss separating the President and his intended constituents—the missing American public—sealed the doom of his health plan, despite what might have been its popular virtues.

The story of President Clinton's call for national service mirrors the lesson taught by health policy, but in reverse. At its best (and it was often at its best), this was an appeal to high citizenship, yet it drew many young people out of self-absorption and privatism without kindling much affection for government among them. Some critics regarded the program as a kind of government-sponsored voluntarism, which seemed to be a contradiction in terms. Others deemed it another expression of an all too familiar self-interest, since service-corps members received educational vouchers and a minimum-wage living allowance as part of their contract. Still others argued that it was a special-interest benefit package for either middle-class college students (who didn't need it) or the disadvantaged (who did but shouldn't have!). Indeed, there has not always been complete agreement within the Corporation for National and Community Service on the relation of citizenship and civil society to service programs.[5]

I will return to the ways that voluntarism exemplifies the differences between our three perspectives on civil society, but it may be said here that national service and community service belong, ideally, neither to the government domain nor to the private sector but to civil society: indeed, it helps to define democratic civil society as a third and independent domain. Yet, because the idea of civil society has been absent from our political consciousness, it has been hard for many Americans to grasp that service is about citizenship in civil society, not about market self-interest or political altruism.

Our understanding of what it means to be a citizen and a politician is transformed by a strong democratic civil society. Without an independent civil sector, politicians too easily mutate into public "professionals" out of touch with their constituencies, while citizens are reduced to being privatized and whining antagonists — or ungrateful clients of government services they readily consume without being willing to pay for. Yet, as Boyte and Kari have insisted, despite the public cynicism of our times, an appetite for civic engagement is still manifest in local activity throughout the United States and, increasingly, in Europe and elsewhere as well. "For all of our problems and fears as a nation, civic energy abounds . . . a rich array of civic work in many diverse settings is evident across the country."[6] What is missing is the space — both literal and metaphoric — for that engagement to take place and be understood. What is missing is a place for us.

William Bennett's *Book of Virtues* compiles many a salutary moral tale, but the virtues it celebrates are produced by neither government nor markets. There is a danger that one might think that the act of buying, let alone reading, the book is somehow tantamount to acquiring the virtues. Yet the virtues Bennett extols belong to traditional communities that no longer exist, and families and civic associations can cultivate them only in the free space of civil society. Character *can* be a source of civic renewal, but commercial markets are just as character-corrupting as government bureaucracies. The communities that communitarians yearn for are not likely to flourish between the crowded freeways and the denuded public squares of an overweening commercial civilization, where corporate developers claim they have won another victory for democracy every time they build a new mall.

What does civil society in the context of a third domain demand of us? How might it be reconstituted to give both citizens and politicians space to act that is neither governmental nor commercial? And time to play and deliberate and interact in a world today where production and consumption seem to demand so much time? Is a civic space imaginable that is neither radically individualistic nor suffocatingly communitarian? A civic dwelling place that is neither a capitol building nor a shopping mall nor a tribal hearthside? These are not rhetorical questions: the denizens of sprawling suburbs, of busted inner cities, of gated communities founded on fear and escapism have to look long and hard to find anything resembling a genuine civic space. Yet, without it, democracy cannot survive.

To imagine how a vigorous, civic republican, civil society looks, we may want to think about the actual places Americans occupy as they go about their daily lives, when they are engaged neither in politics (voting, jury service, paying taxes) nor in commerce (working for pay, producing, shopping, consuming). Such activities include going to church or synagogue or mosque, doing volunteer work, participating in a civic association, supporting a philanthropy, joining a fraternal organization, contributing to a charity, working in a parent-teacher group or neighborhood watch or hospital fund-raising society, or joining with neighbors to clean up a local park and, of course, engaging in family affairs. All these civic engagements occur in spaces we share for purposes other than government or commerce. They share with the private sector the gift of liberty: we go to them voluntarily and join in them as freely associated individuals and groups. But unlike private sector associations, these groups afford common ground and collaborative modes of action and have a public feel without being coercive; they permit voluntary activity that is not, however, privatized.

Strong democratic civil society is marked by a form of association richer and thicker than contractual market relations but not so binding as the kinship (ascriptive) relations of the ideal *Gemeinschaft* community. The clansman has all the virtues of the blood brother but also the limitations of the bondsman—he is, literally, bound! The consumer has the virtues of the autonomous freeman but the limitations of the deracinated solitary—he is alone! Civil society's ideal citizen mediates between these virtues and vices: she is not so steeped in the consolations of solidarity as the clansman but is much freer; she is less radically autonomous than the consumer but better able to enjoy the comforts of neighborly social relations. Her civic activities may feel more "artificial" than those in a natural kinship community, but they are far more "natural" than what draws her as a shopper to a mall or as a voter to a polling station.

Social scientists often categorize traditional civic institutions—foundations, schools, churches, public-interest groups, voluntary associations, civic groups, social movements, not to mention the family—as simply "private." But it is in the neighborhood civil domain that they belong. Although they are nongovernmental, they are public. There are many of them, and by no means just in the United States. The authors of *The New Civic Atlas* note that "the rise of civil society around the globe is unmistakable and inspiring," and believe that it promises a "massive, almost universal movement toward greater citizen participation and influence."[7] This hyperbole is no doubt in large part wishful thinking, but it is given some credibility by the fact that sixty countries report striking growth in NGOs, foundations, and civic associations in the last ten years. Hungary, which before the Second World War had a strong civil-society tradition, is typical. Where less than ten years ago (in 1989) it had fewer than 400 foundations and 8,500 civic associations, Hungary today boasts of more than 15,000 foundations and nearly 30,000 civic associations, many created as a consequence of crucial changes in the civil code between 1987 and 1993.[8] In many of the surveyed countries, civic association remains closely tied to the church and its political party counterparts, but there is also a growth in secular associations and in transnational associations as well.

In the United States, myriad forms of association include religious powerhouses like the United Jewish Federation and the Federation of Catholic Charities (religious giving accounts for by far the largest proportion of charitable giving in America), but also smaller groups that have influence well beyond their size. These include organizations such as American Health Decisions, the Industrial Areas Foundation (from Saul Alinsky to Ernie Cortez), the Oregon Health Parliament, the National Issues Forums of the Kettering Foundation, the Study Circles Movement, policy juries, and televoting and deliberative video town meetings. James Fishkin, of the University of Texas, has organized weekend televised town meetings in which citizens deliberate on policy controversies (often changing their minds in rational ways), and the political scientist Thedore Becker has pioneered deliberative televoting experiments in Hawaii, California, and elsewhere.[9] These and other practical, ongoing experiments in deliberation and consensus-building suggest that there is a broad range of activities which are voluntary rather than identity-based, and which create association around common activity rather than common history. Forging these new voluntarist associations opens up the public spaces closed down by the erosion of thicker communitarian associations. Familes have of course a powerful biological basis, but as social groups they, too, are forged by common activities and shared experience. Moreover, these activities engage citizens who meet and act on public goods even though they do not regard themselves as public officials or government professionals. In debating their shared aspirations as well as their conflicting interests, they effectively establish the civic space that I call strong democratic civil society.

The media, too, where and when they favor their public responsibilities over their commercial ambitions, can be understood as part of civil society rather than in the private sector. Democratic theory has traditionally interpreted the media as crucial to a civil society, since they afford us free communication and diversified information. But (theory and practice intersect here) when the free activities of the media, like those of other civil associations we think of as civic, cannot find room between an expansive government sector and a hegemonic market sector, they are relegated to the merely "private" sphere, and we come then to regard them as private, primarily commercial. And then, no surprise, they behave like jackals. For privatization and commercialization are driving the media in the wrong direction. Sports and news bureaus are being integrated in many media businesses, and in television the hard walls separating news and entertainment (in shows like *Hard Copy* or even *Sixty Minutes* nowadays) as well as advertising and information (in the extended infomercials shown everywhere) are coming down. The blurring of the line between journalism and commercialism is particularly apparent at the *Los Angeles Times*, which recently reorganized internally by pairing particular news departments with their advertising and promotion counterparts, on the theory that reporters and editors who understand the financial and commercial constraints on their sections might be better able to compete in Los Angeles's media-saturated metropolis. This may be good business, but, if the aim is civic integrity and journalistic autonomy, it makes for questionable journalism. Supporters of the *Times* experiment will rightly note that newspapers are in desperate straits and require radical reform if they are to survive. Survival, however, may require that civil society is once more compromised. In this same way, privatization has meant that certain traditional liberal activities concerned with the public environment, public-safety rules, full employment, and other social goods lose their public-interest status and reappear as private-sector "special-interest groups," and they behave and are treated in much the same way as for-profit corporations and private-interest associations with much narrower goals. To return to the earlier example, journalists become communication- and information-industry employees with more responsibility to shareholder profits than to the competence of their fellow citizens. Under these circumstances, President Clinton's alleged sexual practices are given more attention than his actual political programs.

I mean to celebrate here the benefits to liberty of a conception of civil society that insists on free and inclusive associations, but I recognize that we pay a price for it. For this conception defines a civil association in ways that may exclude forms of community which sociologists deem central to associative life. As Michael Walzer has prudently observed, while the "greatest virtue" of free association "lies in its inclusiveness . . . inclusiveness does not make for heroism. 'Join the associations of your choice' is not a slogan to rally political militants."[10] To insist on inclusion as a key criterion for democratic forms of community is, ironically, to define civil society non-inclusively! Not every community meets the standard. For example, communitarians place family and religion at the center of civil society and are understandably reluctant to imagine family and religious groups as being outside that society, even though the liberal majority may deem them (in at least some forms) undemocratic, inegalitarian, or hierarchical. We may not like the goals or autocratic structure of, say, a religious cult or the Ku Klux Klan or a Montana militia unit, but as voluntary membership groups these must surely be included in a "neutral" conception of civil society — or so a consistent sociologist would argue. Biting the bullet, advocates of strong democratic civil society acknowledge that they are less than neutral: their conception of civil society is a rather restricted subset of all possible forms of association, and they limit it to forms that are at least nominally or potentially democratic and open.

Families are obviously the building blocks of every extended form of human association. Traditional political philosophers often thought of the state itself as a form of extended family, in which the sovereign acted as paterfamilias to his subjects. Religion, a social glue stronger than any other, also seems indispensable to civil society at its most general. Strong democrats nevertheless remain skeptics here, however reluctantly. Though they may wish to incorporate the powerful binding forces of family and church into their conception of civil society, they dare not do so without qualifying both, just as they qualify every other form of civic association. The groups in a strong democratic civil society must be open and inclusive (and thus include the right of exit as well as free entry) and must enforce some degree of equality among their members. Other less inclusive groups certainly qualify as generically social, but if they are to count as part of a rigorously defined democratic *civil* society they need to be more than that. Otherwise, the modifier "civil" loses its meaning. The Nation of Islam, for example, may be a genuine community, but it may fail the test of democratic civil society and fall into the circle of viable (even vital) associations that define America's associative life more generally.

Democrats recognize that in speaking of *civil* society they are speaking not of any old kind of society, but of one that stipulates public and democratic conditions. Strong democratic civil society is profoundly normative. It gains its democratic character at the cost of a limited compass, and maintains its civility by insisting on forms of association that may in fact exclude generically social ones. The objective formal criteria for these forms of association are related not to their political coloration but to the nature of their membership and institutional architecture. These criteria are subject to constant reconsideration and revision, being less than wholly scientific but more than expressions of irrational private preference.

The Nation of Islam, to return to this example, may offer its African-American members a vibrant sense of identity they are unlikely to find elsewhere, but to the degree that it defines itself by its enemies (Jews? Christians? whites?) and is so strictly hierarchical, it may fall outside this definition of civil society. Still, if its separatism and racial exclusivity are but part of a long-term developmental strategy aimed at the economic and cultural integration of African-Americans into a more democratic America, and it makes its peace over time with those it once denounced as "enemies," its future might yet be congruent with that of democratic civil society. Civility itself is a flexible construct, and democracy has a broad application. Religions that do not claim theocratic sovereignty in the secular world and cults whose membership is genuinely voluntary can meet democratic criteria, especially relaxed ones, just as families which are open and egalitarian in the long term because they assure equality among the various roles within them (even when those roles are distinctive), and which eventually produce autonomous adults (even if by less than democratic means), are sufficiently democratic to be judged "civil." Degree is everything here, and true democrats should render judgment case by case.

In fact, so crucial are forms of association like families and religion to the coherence and solidarity of society that strong democrats have good reason to nurture and support them even if they fail the test of democratic civility. Ideally, support should be directed at making them more open and democratic, but unless family and religion perdure, democratic or not, civil society suffers. Their erosion in this century is to some extent beyond redress, the consequence of modernizing forces that no social tinkering can reverse. To the extent population declinists like Nicholas Eberstadt are right, the very idea of family may be in doubt, since for many people in what he predicts will be the coming population implosion, " 'family' would be understood as a unit that does not include any biological contemporaries or peers."[11] Legislation cannot avert such a future and in any case such nouveaux families are not likely to be sources of traditionally defined family values. But speculation aside, to the extent social policy makes a difference today, democrats frequently seem to be, from my civil society perspective, on the wrong side of the argument. Understandably intolerant of patriarchy, they will oppose new family-friendly ideas tout court—ideas like covenant marriage or the traditional morality behind the Promise Keepers.

Yet covenant marriage, as it has been legislatively enacted in Louisiana, does not replace no-fault divorce; it permits couples who seek deeper forms of commitment voluntarily to enter into a mildly coercive contract that requires them to wait two years rather than six months to divorce, and admonishes them to seek counseling before starting and before ending a marriage. Secularists worried about the Christian overtones of "covenant," and anxious about placing impediments before women who may want to escape abusive marriages, refuse to acknowledge either the importance of moral bonds or the possible utility of reinforcing them with legislative sanctions. Nonetheless, in this case Louisiana has struck a balance, underwriting family values without circumscribing freedom (no fault remains an option for everyone).

The Promise Keepers allow men who fear they may have failed their families to repledge themselves to fidelity, non-violence and responsibility. These are norms that can certainly be made to conform to patriarchy (though they would seem to recommend rather than condemn it!), but they are also compatible with egalitarian constructions of family life and opposed to the kinds of violent irresponsibility that—without enhancing anybody's liberty—engender abuse and wreck the family. Advocates of an unachievable "best" seem here to be making war on betterment.

Government may also have good reason, from the perspective of a strong democratic civil society, to pull back from the enforced secularism that courts have ruled is required if we are to honor the separation of church and state. In my reading, to bar the government from establishing a state religion does not require that government forbid religious expression in civil society. To believe that it should is to confound civil society and government. Government may not order a crèche onto the commons, but does this mean it is obliged to order a crèche (or a Star of David) off the commons? Are religious displays in civil society synonymous with government-sponsored religion? By distinguishing civil society from both the commercial and the state sectors, we create a place where people may be permitted to express the communal dimension of their beliefs without being guilty of establishing a state religion.

There is something narrow and myopic about the broad secular insistence that if we are to respect the separation of church and state, religion must be wholly private and personal. The Bible is not a novel and the Torah is not philosophy that one enjoys privately while affirming the rights of others to their own privacy. Religion is by its very nature communal, and its practice is possible only in common space and public places. The separation of church and state was intended to protect religion, not destroy it. In forbidding worship in public spaces we risk forbidding worship; and when we argue that worship is constitutional only when conducted privately, away from the commons, we stumble into hypocrisy.

The task of balancing liberty of conscience and variety of belief with the necessarily public (but not governmental) character of religion is without a doubt arduous. As with all such exercises in civic balancing, it is easy to go wrong — in both directions. Traditional civic permissiveness that encouraged school prayer and the public display of religious icons in common spaces with no thought to the sensibilities of minority belief systems probably tipped the balance too much in favor of the majority religion. But today's insistence on banishing religion altogether—and not just from the government sphere but from civil society altogether—tips it too much in favor of a dogmatic and (as it appears to believers) coercive secularism. To protect the sensibilities of some, we make common religious worship difficult for many; but common religion entails religion in the commons and some accommodation to its public character has to be made. To ensure variety, we banish from civil society the kinds of common symbols that help hoop together society's fragmentary identities—and then we complain that common morality and civic responsibility have disappeared from public life. Can we shift the balance back a little without re-creating that single monolithic sect Adam Smith feared could destroy civil society? It is certainly true that religion and family are not so vulnerable that circumscribing their civic compass will ruin them. Yet civil society is not so fragile that its autonomy and variety are destroyed the moment its boundaries are extended to include family life and worship, even in their more traditional manifestations. Especially if we can guarantee pluralism.

This said, it remains true that strong democratic civil society must be more narrowly defined and more explicitly prescriptive than other notions of civil society. It acknowledges the family and religion as indispensable to civil society, but sets conditions that are more demanding than those of its libertarian cousin and certainly less family-friendly and church-friendly than its communitarian cousin. This allows it to mediate between communitarian and libertarian notions, however, neither too thick (the danger of traditional community) nor too thin (the danger of the market-place).

Accepting the strong democratic perspective has palpable consequences for how we conduct our civic lives. Consider the example of voluntary service introduced briefly above. Voluntarism would seem to be a perfect exemplar of civil society: voluntary activity on behalf of the public good and the community by individuals discharging their civic obligations. But exactly how one understands its meaning and place in the political world depends very much on how one thinks of civil society. If, for example, you regard civil society as synonymous with the private sector and with the contractual relations of the market economy, voluntarism is a strictly private affair. People treat service to others as a gift, plain charity. In the language of Presidents Reagan and Bush, servers are "heroes" or "points of light" acting not so much as citizen volunteers but as private persons taking up a social slack. When one thinks of it this way, voluntary service privatizes government and makes voluntarism not a bridge to democracy but a substitute for it. The implicit message seems to be: We do not need democratic government to solve our problems, we can do it ourselves, one by one. Where public institutions fail, private voluntary activity will succeed.

Voluntarism in this perspective is less a recipe than a substitute for good citizenship. It may even be used politically to underscore the alleged bankruptcy of the welfare state (since government programs have miscarried, let charities and churches feed the hungry and house the homeless!) and the defects of public schools or teachers' unions (let a million volunteer readers teach literacy to a generation of children whom public-school teachers have failed!). Far from repairing the breach between governed and governors, voluntary service understood this way widens the gulf, teaching lessons about self-sufficiency and independence rather than about cooperation and interdependence. The rhetoric of individual philanthropy displaces the more democratic rhetoric of reciprocal obligations and civic responsibility. Volunteers "reach out" and "reach down" to the needy to "rescue" them—as General Colin Powell's well-meaning use of such language at the Philadelphia Voluntarism Summit in the spring of 1997 unfortunately suggested.

The communitarian approach to voluntarism, in contrast, puts a welcome emphasis on the obligations of community membership, and it softens the highly individualistic notion of service that is preferred by liberals with a market point of view. Groups and individuals have obligations to serve: one speaks of corporate responsibility and the obligations owed by families and membership associations to their neighborhoods and regions. Communitarianism thus moves beyond heroic individualism, but it stops short of political citizenship. Its rhetoric is moralizing and supererogatory, calling on us to discharge duties that go beyond reciprocity, contract, or anything we can be said to "owe" our neighbors as fellow citizens. The communitarian version of voluntarism steps out of individual self-sufficiency without stepping into citizenship.

Voluntarism in the strong democratic perspective, however, treats service volunteers and the people they serve, too, as citizens. The idea is not that one is ennobling those who serve or rescuing those who are served but that one is empowering both, facilitating and advancing self-governance. Never do for others, says the prudent volunteer, what they can do for themselves. President Clinton came to office in 1992 with a strong, distinctly democratic rhetoric of service and voluntarism. The primary social experiment he fashioned, the Corporation for National and Community Service (now simply the Corporation for National Service), aimed to transform the market ethic of private voluntarism into a civic ethic of citizenship. Aware of the brooding distrust that divided many Americans from their government—the growing alienation that the sociologist Robert Putnam spotlighted in his essay "Bowling Alone"—the President seemed to make a case against "serving alone" and for "serving together."

His approach involved three important innovations, each intended to expand purely private visions of voluntarism and give them a civic aspect. The first was to link service explicitly to education, making education vouchers the primary reward for people who enlisted in Americorps. We have to be educated for service, and service itself is an education for citizenship. We are not born citizens but must learn the skills and arts of liberty (thus, the "liberal arts"), in what Tocqueville called the ongoing, extremely arduous "apprenticeship of liberty." Putting learning and service together was not just a convenience or some hypocritical form of "paid voluntarism" but an expression of their essential connection (the Corporation has a program called "Learn and Serve").

The second innovation was to treat the service volunteers of the Corporation's several programs as members of neither the governmental nor the private sector but of autonomous civil society, hence as emblems of the partnership among the federal government, the several states, and local communities. Service volunteers would sign up for a national program, yet they would serve in regional and local programs coordinated by autonomous state commissions in cooperation with private charities and civic associations. Americorps volunteers were thus intended to be human bridges spanning federal and local, public and private, civic and personal agencies. They would define a democratic civil space. Their service, at once both local and national, would empower them as responsible citizens as well as benefit the communities where they worked.

The third innovation was that the form of service measurably affected not only the communities it served (count up the kids tutored or the homeless who were sheltered) but the volunteers themselves, educating them in responsibility and preparing them for citizenship. In the first "summer of service" in 1993, President Clinton said that a season of service could lead to a lifetime of citizenship: every volunteer was a prospective citizen, every citizen a partisan of democracy. Volunteers are of course heroes of a sort, but, finally, democracy is government without heroes, government by ordinary women and men taking responsibility for their lives. Voluntary community service in a civil society is thus a training

ground of citizenship. Like military and other forms of citizen service, it yields useful benefits for society and educates women and
men into citizenship. It may approximate that elusive "moral
equivalent of war" that William James sought as a forge for citizenship that did not depend on killing. Ideally, formal voluntarism,
like formal schooling, should be temporary, and it becomes superfluous once everyone is self-governing. Like democratic founders,
strong democratic volunteers will their own extinction. They meta-
morphose into citizens who create a society in which, because
everyone shares in obligatory responsibilities, there is no longer any
need for discretionary "volunteers."

Even at its civic best, voluntarism shares the limits of localism.
We live in a world of multinational corporations, global environmental and communication ecosystems, and transnational economic and cultural forces. We cannot solve, one by one and
locally, the big infrastructural social problems created over a half
century by national and transnational power. One of the paradoxes
of democratic engagement is that while participation is by definition local (we participate bottom up and locally through processes
that are naturally centrifugal), power is by definition central (force
rules top down and centrally through processes that are naturally
centripetal). Volunteer cleanup crews in Chicago's Hyde Park or
Paris's St.-Denis suburb cannot stop global warming any more than
volunteer tax accountants working with Korean grocers in Brooklyn
or Turkish construction workers in Berlin can redress the Asian
currency crisis. The doors that open to civic engagement are in
the neighborhoods, but the rooms where power is exercised are in
the commercial capitals and global metropolises. How do we build
a civic house that incorporates them both?

Civic voluntarism is a start, as long as it is not regarded as a
terminus. Vibrant forms of local engagement can catalyze participation in politics at the national level, just as we can begin our
journey to the anonymous global city by acknowledging social re-

sponsibility and citizenship in the neighborhood. At its best, that is exactly what voluntarism as a feature of civic socialization achieves. But we will also have to find a place for appropriate national and global civic activity.

The effect that local participation has on power is also conditioned by the difference between decentralizing power and privatizing it. When government devolves responsibility to local government and to citizens in the way we associate with federalism, it shares authority, empowers the neighborhood, and encourages local civic responsibility. When it withdraws from responsibility and privatizes power, it turns away from accountability and responsibility altogether, trusting in market forces defined by self-interest to take good care of the public interests it has abandoned. In the first instance, it shares power; in the second, it abjures power. It is a robust government devoted to federalism that decentralizes power and forges government–civil society partnerships, asking volunteers to act as citizens who share with their government the responsibility for solving public local problems and forging common neighborhood interests. It is a slack and irresponsible government that privatizes power, asking volunteers to do by themselves all the things governments are elected to do and that individuals, however good-willed, lack the resources to do.

A government that shares responsibility through decentralizing power acts as a facilitator and instrument of civil society: an entity that nourishes, protects, and encourages robust civic activity and, when the central character of power and the national or global character of problems demand it, acts on behalf of the citizenry. Democratic central government is, in other words, civil society organized for common action. It is civil society when it picks up its law code and straps on its pistol and, legitimized and authorized by its popular mandate, becomes the sovereign. Government is civil society's common arm, just as civil society is government's animating body.

Above all, it is this critical relationship between participation and power that leads me to favor the strong democratic idea of civil society over its two rivals. The strong democratic idea allows civil society to reemerge as a mediating, civic republican domain between the overgrown governmental and the metastasizing private sectors, between the thin liberal conception of citizenship (which "cannot inspire the sense of community and civic engagement that liberty requires," as Sandel puts it) and the thick but dense and suffocating communitarian identity (which endangers liberty and equality). Moreover, strong democracy does this without further alienating citizens from their democratic governing institutions or assailing government as something wholly foreign to civil society.

Critics of big government think the only way to shrink it is to cede power and privilege to the private sector, but this abdication of power and public responsibility means either privatization, with heroic individuals and responsible corporations taking on the entire burden of the public weal, or a surrender to hegemonic communitarian parochialism, with communities inflicting their values and social relations on everything. By the same token, critics of the market sector believe that the only way to regulate and contain its corruptions is to expand government, but while this will certainly help to regulate monopolies and to domesticate private power (worthy causes!), it can encroach on civic turf if too zealous. As Edmund Burke, that worthy eighteenth-century critic of legalism, noticed long ago, if we rely exclusively on the police and the courts to instill an ethos of law and order in society, we may discover that our communities cannot sustain that ethos on their own.

During the last three decades, like progressives and conservatives everywhere, Democrats and Republicans in the United States have drawn their battle lines in a war between the state and the private sector. The Democrats, although they talk about ending big government, still defend it, understanding that it is needed to do battle against corporatism, and hoping against hope they can "reinvent" it, and render it less alienating and inefficient. The Republicans, acknowledging the need for some minimalist government, exhort not decentralization but privatization at every turn, even when it compromises the very moral and civic ideals to which they are traditionally committed (family values, religious norms, civic liberty) and which the federal government has helped to instill through public education, national service, and codes of public decency. When Republican inclinations to communitarian cultural conservatism clash with Republican proclivities to free market liberalism, civic republicanism suffers. Weighing the claims of moral interventionism and economic laissez-faire, Irving Kristol once settled for "Two Cheers for Capitalism." Nowadays, in the wake of the triumph of market liberalism, it's three cheers for the market and morality be hanged. Cultural conservatives like Ralph Reed and Patrick Buchanan and William Bennett, along with more progressive communitarians like Alasdair MacIntyre, Charles Taylor, and Mary Ann Glendon, complain about this, and they have gotten a hearing in intellectual circles,[12] but Republican politics do not change much.

In Europe, those on the right who are searching for what a half century ago was called "moral rearmament" have turned from traditional laissez-faire parties to nationalist ones, where they mobilize zealous opponents of both the liberal state and the liberal economy. And so we are locked in a zero-sum game in which, it seems, the government cannot protect justice or enforce morals without diminishing liberty and enjoining dependency, while the private sector cannot support freedom or protect privacy without diminishing equality, promoting commercialism, and annihilating the commonweal.

Civic freedom is clearly served by neither of these alternatives. But political parties in the West—and increasingly in Asia, Latin

America, and the Third World—are confronted with a Hobson's choice between a kind of caricatured Big Brother government, which affords some distributive justice but risks tyranny and dependency, and a kind of caricatured runaway free market, which secures negative liberty but fosters monopoly, inequality, and social injustice. Within the confines of so wrenching a dichotomy, the democratic liberty produced by civic engagement and a common life is overshadowed by the negative liberty sought by people who distrust civic and common power. Especially in ex-communist nations, people are reluctant to strengthen state controls even in the name of democracy and justice. After all, that was the rationale of the people's republics, too. But with the market as the only alternative, there seem to be few citizen-friendly choices—hence the flight to nationalism, xenophobia, and revanchist communism.

Citizens can hardly be happy with this choice. For they sense that democracy is precisely that form of government in which not politicians and bureaucrats but an empowered people use legitimate force to put flesh on the bones of its liberty, in which liberty carries with it the obligations of social responsibility and citizenship as well as the rights of legal persons, in which rights and responsibilities are two aspects of a civic identity that belongs neither to state bureaucrats nor to private consumers but to citizens alone.

Civil society is in fact *the* domain of citizens. It can place limits on government without ceding public goods to the private sphere, and at the same time it can dissipate the atmosphere of solitariness and greed that surrounds markets without suffocating in big government's exhaust fumes or in the stifling air of would-be natural communities. Both government and the private sector can and should be humbled by the growth of civil society, for it absorbs some of the public aspirations of government (its commitment to public work) without being coercive, and it maintains liberty without yielding to the jungle anarchy of commercial markets. Reinvigorated civil society can thus rehabilitate democratic government in the Western nations, whose citizens now hold it in ill-repute, and it can create a ground for democratization that does not remind people of the intrusive totalitarian past in nations where the state is still associated with the taint of enduring historical abuses.

Finally, strong democratic civil society invokes civic faith to sustain vanishing religious faith and common mores. We might yearn for the solidarity of a traditional blood community or the common values of a homogenous society that resembles Braveheart's colorfully monochrome Scotland or Joan of Arc's united France. We live, however, in societies that have been striated by successive waves of immigration and the rising tides of global labor in constant motion. Germany is nearly ten percent foreign and is becoming a reluctant "melting pot."[13] Five million Muslims live permanently in Catholic France, while the United States measured by its population under twenty-five is already a country of myriad minorities but no majority at all. Even were it compatible with freedom, blood can no longer bind the national community together—not here in America, not anywhere.

Civic faith, what the German social philosopher Jürgen Habermas calls constitutional patriotism, is the only available social glue, thin as it sometimes feels. Richard Rorty is sure that in our thin liberal societies today this glue "consists in little more than a consensus that the point of social organization is to let everybody have a chance at self-creation to the best of his or her abilities, and that goal requires . . . the standard 'bourgeois freedoms.' "[14] But I think Abraham Lincoln was much closer to the mark. In his 1858 July 4 Speech, he proposed that in an immigrant society moral sentiment might do the work of blood and do it well. When Americans not descended directly from the founders "look back through . . . history to trace their connection with those [founding] days by blood, they find they have none," Lincoln acknowledged. Nonetheless, when they "look through that old Declaration of Independence they find that those old men say that 'we hold these truths to be self-evident, that all men are created equal,' and . . . that moral sentiment . . . is the father of all moral principle in them, and . . . they have a right to claim it as though they were blood of the blood, and flesh of the flesh, of men who wrote that Declaration, and so they are." We, too—we Americans of a hundred ethnic origins, we French who share at most a common language, we Nigerians of the many different tribes, we Muslims of scores of nationalities—we, too, have the right to claim civic principle as if we were blood of the blood and pledge common principle as if we were flesh of the flesh, for in claiming and pledging in this manner, we are bonded together in a society that sets us free.

To re-create civil society on the model of strong democracy does not entail a novel civic architecture, at least in many Western nations; rather, civil society requires us to reconceptualize and reposition the institutions already in place. Where a civic sector already exists, we must deploy civic strategies and laws to give it room to grow and flourish. Where it exists only as an ideal, we must suggest strategies that help to seed civic institutions and then help them to grow. And where it is entirely absent (in the international sector), it must be invented anew.

These must be strategies that permit schools, foundations, community movements, the media, and other civil associations to reclaim a public voice and political legitimacy in the face of cynics who write them off as hypocritical special interests. I hope to give the otherwise abstract idea of a public voice a real place, an actual geography, somewhere other than in the atlas of government. Finally, I will suggest, government is essential in helping to create civic space, in protecting it from bureaucratic encroachment (whether public or private), and in nurturing its animating discourse. If democratic civil society is the sine qua non of democratic government, democratic government is the indispensable condition of its flourishing. Middle Europe's fledgling democratic institutions are struggling because they are without a foundation in a nurturing civil society, which is missing because of the long history of undemocratic governance in that region. Unsurprisingly, the most successful new democracy in the domain of former Soviet influence is the Czech Republic, which has had the longest experience with civil society. As Petr Pajas observes, "In the 19th century, the tradition of citizen participation in the Republic of Czechoslovakia was established with a national social revival. Civil society flourished, with charitable, health, and social care activities organized by the Catholic Church and several independent foundations."[15] Following the revolution of 1989 and a half century of civil-society decline, poet-President Vaclav Hável turned his dissident's dream of a civil society into a program of civic laws, including Acts on the Right of Assembly, on Associations of Civilians, and on Churches and Religious Congregations and on Public Benefit Corporations, resulting in today's (comparatively) lustrous Czech civil society, a sector that continues to grow despite the onset of malaise in the Republic's stalled political sector.

When I have completed the examination of legislative and practical proposals, I will consider two crucial functions that a revitalized civil society fills in a world of democratized government and civilized markets: how it provides communicative civility and discursive commonalty, even when the political arena is fragmentary and hyper-diverse; and how it provides space for meaningful public work even when robotization and innovations in information technology threaten an eventual end of private work. It is ironic that our modern world, having deprived democratic civic institutions of a proper time and place, may now be compelled to ask those very institutions to rescue it from materialism, market totalism, and the growing disparity between productivity (ever rising) and jobs (ever diminishing).

3

MAKING CIVIL SOCIETY REAL:
PRACTICAL STRATEGIES

We have seen, in our study of civil society thus far, that there are three obstacles to civil society as the mediating domain between the government and the private sector: government itself, when it is arrogant and overweening; market dogmas, when they presume that private individuals and groups can secure public goods; and the yearning for community, when it subordinates liberty and equality to solidarity.

As to the first, the tendency of all institutions to ossify and become distanced from their constituents (the so-called iron law of oligarchy) turns government representatives into enemies of their citizens and, eventually, makes even democratically elected governments rigid and hierarchical, with the representatives regarding themselves as the sole civic actors on the political scene, governing on behalf of citizens instead of facilitating citizen self-government. When that happens, the democratic citizenry in whose name the governments govern is actually disempowered, at once both dependent and alienated.

As to the second, the myth of the invisible hand encourages

market enthusiasts to believe that privatization is a synonym for democratization and empowerment, and for civic liberty to flourish, one need only get government out of the way. But the results are quite otherwise: an eclipse of the public, a one-dimensional culture of privatism and greed, and an addictive materialism that turns autonomous citizens into dependent consumers.

As for the third, the communitarian thirst for the restoration of lost values and value communities encourages people to impose on others their own cultural values through either government or quasi-censorious institutions of civil society. In the resulting solidaristic community, insiders favor identity over equality as the most precious of all social values and everyone else is left feeling like outsiders.

Ironically, although government itself has recently been seen as part of the problem, it has an opportunity here to be part of the solution. For a disciplined, self-limiting government can behave modestly. Such modesty is characteristic of President Clinton's new Democrats (prompted by the Democratic Leadership Council's Progressive Policy Institute), Tony Blair's "New" Labor Party, and Lionel Jospin's new socialists. Yet these new progressives do trust government to help ameliorate the crushing effects of monopoly corporations and counter their imposition of commercial uniformity and cultural homogenization. Through its courts and legal system government can also assure that liberty is protected against corrosive side effects of the all-too-human longing for solidarity.

The true enemy of civil society is, in fact, neither government nor corporations per se, but bureaucracy, dogmatism, unresponsiveness, totalism, bloat, unaccountability, absolutism, and inertia wherever they are found. While laissez-faire obsessives are loath to admit it, these defects are unfortunately found as much in private commerce as in the government, among firms and fraternities no less than in welfare bureaucracies. Had President Clinton announced not the "end of big government" but the "end of Leviathan, the end of big bureaucratic bloat," he would have declared war more symmetrically on the ills that afflict us. That he did not and that he has shown so little appetite to address the private sector attests to its intimidating power (as well as its campaign finance leverage).

Where government is at fault, laws must help it move to self-limitation and reform; and where the private sector is the problem, government must be the public's ally in curbing commercial and market abuses, and in forbidding the moral encroachments that comformist communities make when they try to impose their own values and way of life on all of us. Ultimately, democratic government is but an extension of the common power of citizens, and citizens must use that common power while working to reform its susceptibility to abuse. Power corrupts, and private power, neither accountable nor, often, even visible, may be much more corrupting (and far less tractable) than the power of democratic government. We can always "throw the buggers out!" when politicians get too big for their britches or forget to whom they are accountable. But there is no recall power against managers of the marketplace when they are not accountable to the sovereign public. That is a lesson worth remembering in an age when government is so disdained and markets so widely celebrated, when the prevailing orthodoxy is so insistently laissez-faire. It is a shameful reminder of the hypocrisy of those who benefit from privatism when they pretend that government has no role in defending those whom privatism cripples.

Democracy is not a synonym for the marketplace, and the notion that by privatizing government we can establish civil society and civic goods is a dishonorable myth. The freedom to buy a Coke or a Big Mac or a video of the Lion King eating a Big Mac is not the freedom to determine how you will live and under what kind of regime. Coke and McDonald's and MTV thrive in undemocratic Singapore and China as well as they do in chaotic, semidemocratic Russia and in the genuinely democratic Czech Republic. Historically, it is not capitalism that produced democracy but democracy that produced capitalism. Capitalism needs democracy but does not know how to create or sustain it, and frequently it produces circumstances that can undermine it.

The myth of the market is our most insidious myth, not just because so many believe it, but because the market's invisible bonds slip on so easily and feel so very much like freedom. Is shopping really a synonym for choice, even when, in a hyper-consumer society, consumption is more addiction than voluntary activity? I have written elsewhere and at length on the disastrous confusion between the moderate, mostly well-founded claim that flexibly regulated markets are the most efficient instruments of economic productivity and wealth accumulation, and the zany, over-blown claim that unregulated markets are the sole means by which we can produce and distribute everything we care about—from durable goods to spiritual values, from capital development to social justice, from profitability to sustainable environments, from private wealth to the essential commonweal. This second claim has moved some people to insist that goods as diverse and obviously public as education, culture, penology, full employment, social welfare, and ecological survival should be handed over to the profit sector for arbitration and disposal, but the argument of this book shows how inadequate and dangerous this misapprehension is.

Markets are simply not designed to do the things democratic polities or free civil societies do. Markets give us private, not public, modes of discourse: we pay as consumers in currencies of consumption to producers of material goods, but we cannot use this currency when we deal with one another as citizens or neighbors about the social consequences of our private market choices. Markets advance individualistic, not social, goals and they encourage us to speak the language of "I want," not the language of "we need." Markets preclude "we" thinking and "we" action of any kind at all, trusting in the power of aggregated individual choices (the "invisible hand") somehow to secure the common good. In the name of diversity and private choice, markets foster a kind of consumer totalism, turning multidimensional citizens into one-dimensional, solitary shoppers. Consumers speak the divisive rhetoric of "me." Citizens invent the common language of "we."

Markets are also contractual rather than communitarian, which means they flatter our solitary egos but leave unsatisfied our yearning for community; they offer durable goods and fleeting dreams but not a common identity or a collective membership. Virulently negative expressions of communitarian solidarity are in fact often reactions to the market's desocializing features. The thinner the market's social nexus, the thicker and more bloody the response to it — and so what I have called McWorld engenders the Jihad that resists it.

Beyond our markets, then, we need the virtues of democracy and the social relations of civil society; and our markets and our ideal of civil society need democracy to survive. Markets are as likely to undermine as to sustain full employment, environmental safety, public health, social safety nets, education, cultural diversity, and real competition. These common goods are the result of common thinking, cooperation, and sharing of the kind democratic civil society makes possible. The task today, in theory no less than in practice, is to reilluminate public space for a civil society in eclipse. Making space for citizens and giving them a civil voice in their affairs must be the goal of all our practical strategies.

A government pledged to give practical support to citizenship and civil society can effectively and legitimately act through legislative initiatives and reform as a positive facilitator of civil society, as a partner of citizens in removing negative governmental obstacles to civil-society practices, and as an ally of civil society in challenging the totalizing, private commercial sector as well as overly zealous communitarian groups whose fraternal ministrations shrink the purview of citizenship.

There is no legislative domain that cannot be reframed and improved by thinking how it might promote civil society. After all, government programs, regulatory policy (or its absence), and political ideology expressed in laws helped to create our present world. The corporation, that dominating leviathan of the private sector, was itself a creature of government and in American law exists as an "artificial person" only through its status under the law. Happily, both Democrats and Republicans have shown some interest in "legislating civil society"—the Clinton Administration in its ongoing fascination with civil society and public-private partnerships, and the Republicans in the legislative agenda offered by Bill Bennett and Senator Dan Coats for government intervention to sustain civic practices.[1] Government agencies like the United States Information Agency, private philanthropies like George Soros's Open Society Institute, and the Institute for Civil Society and Civicus (the international NGO umbrella organization) all try to strengthen civil society in transitional societies and in the international arena. Some programs are obviously more easily enacted than others. I would propose six possible areas where innovative and liberating laws could nourish civil society without incurring unreasonable new operating costs. In many cases, the new tactics would build on legislative strategies that are already in place (e.g., campaign finance reform, free TV time for candidates, using new telecommunication technologies for the public weal); in others, they could embody new initiatives. The consequences not just of an absence of government intervention but of maladroit and destructive government policy need to be addressed afresh.

In every case, the specific initiatives I suggest here aim to reorient and reconceptualize our policy goals so as to downplay government as an end in itself or as the direct solution to social problems, and to emphasize it as a facilitating instrument of citizens who want to get their own public work done. Far from disappearing, government is strengthened—but by turning it back into what it should always be in a democracy: the agent and instrument of highest resort for the highest and most general objectives of civil society and free citizens; the entity that expresses the "we" of our commonalty; civil society in its legislative mode. The aim is to remove rather than reinforce barriers between the people as a citizenry and their government as their sovereign voice.

Here are six pertinent arenas for legislative action in support of civil society:

1. Enlarging and reinforcing public spaces: specifically, retrofitting commercial malls as multi-use and thus genuinely public spaces.

2. Fostering civic uses of new telecommunications and information technologies, preventing commercialization from destroying their civic potentials: specifically, a civic Internet; public-access cable television; a check on mass-media advertising for (and the commercial exploitation of) children.

3. Domesticating and democratizing production in the global economy: protecting the labor market, challenging disemployment practices; making corporations responsible members of civil society without surrendering the government's regulatory authority.

4. Domesticating and democratizing consumption in the global economy: protecting just wage policies, workplace safety, and the environment; the labeling and/or boycotting of goods produced without regard for safety, environment, or child-labor laws.

5. National and community service, service learning programs, and citizen-nurturing voluntarism.

6. Cultivating the arts and humanities as an indispensable foundation for a free, pluralistic society; treating artists as citizens and citizens as artists in government-supported arts education and service programs.

PUBLIC SPACES

In our mostly privatized, suburbanized world, there are not enough physical places where citizenship can be easily exercised and civil society's free activities can be pursued. Citizens need physical spaces where they can interact and work to solve public problems. "The trouble with socialism," Oscar Wilde once quipped, "is that it takes up too many free evenings." Civil society and its activities encroach on Wednesday afternoons and Saturday mornings, too. And they require space and place. There can be no civic activity without a palpable civic geography. Ducks, to be ducks, need their pond, and the public needs its town square.

Traditionally, town squares, village greens, general stores, city parks, community halls — even barbershops, post offices, water-coolers, and saloons — have been places for informal civic inter-action: neighborly conversation, political argument, the search for shared ground. But when more than half of us now live in sub-urban developments that are anything but neighborhoods and that have no obvious public spaces — neither civic centers nor even sidewalks — or in inner cities where public space is often unsavory or unsafe, we have fewer and fewer of these formal and informal meeting places. In the suburbs, people go almost everywhere by car, and often bank and eat without leaving those cars. Suburban-ization follows the automobile and the kinds of mobility that attend economic development; and there is good reason to think, in the absence of alternatives, that all the world may one day be New Jersey.

In New Jersey, the commonly available public spaces are com-mercial malls, designed to encourage and facilitate purchasing, in-deed, to make material consumption a habit. Stores cater not to traditional needs (try to find a hardware store or dry cleaners or pharmacy in a mall!) but to the manufactured needs of the post-modern economy. Boutiques and novelty chains (The Nature

Store, The Sharper Image, the Disney Store, Brookstone's) prolif-
erate. Even food is proffered like fuel in "food court" pit stops that
maximize caloric intake and minimize the time spent fueling up
for more shopping.

Meanwhile, more traditional urban milieus have been mauled
and malled by architects who think of Las Vegas (or Disneyland)
as an opportunity to do a Times Square theme park, and of Times
Square as an opportunity to bring Las Vegas to New York. In Washington, D.C., Union Station and the old Post Office are examples
of traditional public spaces that have been recast as commercial
spaces. (Ironically, the National Endowments for the Arts and the
Humanities are sequestered upstairs in the commercialized old
Post Office.) Might not both buildings have been refurbished to
include civic and social space as well as shops? Public space means
more than the accidental open areas left behind in cavernous
buildings after commercialization has run its course. Even airports
are coming to resemble malls with airplanes.

If our world is to be malled, is it possible to transform malls into
usable civic spaces? Is an architecture geared to commerce malleable enough to permit alterations to fulfill civic needs? How
might malls be designed and developers encouraged to make space
for neighborhood health clinics, speakers' corners, child-care centers? for political and community meeting spaces, community the-
aters and art galleries, charitable organizations? for information and
media groups and other civic associations? What kind of incentives
might governments offer to make this happen? Could zoning regulations be used to make developers take a more civic approach?
Might "curb cut" permits (which let developers have rights-of-way
from public highways) do the same thing? Why not a "model"
civic-mall competition sponsored by the National Endowment for
the Humanities? A contest for architects to design model civic
space?

Celebration, the Disney Corporation's "new-town" in central

Florida, suggests a new architecture of public space, but it looks more like a mall-plus-homesites than the traditional town its architecture tries to ape. It is a kind of perfect counterparadigm to what I am talking about. It has taken the principles of comic-book spectatorship—sanitized vacations, safety-conscious adventure, vicarious history, homogenized variety, and simulated ethnicity—from their entertainment venue and applied them to a living environment that simulates a "public" from which it is in fact insulated in the manner of the gated community. It is but a short hop from Celebration to Orlando, a real city, but Celebration is as far away from the dark side of the public square—unemployment, welfare poverty, race bias, grand larceny, rape, and murder—as it can get. It is about "a signature golf course, tennis courts, acres of parks, ponds, and open spaces" as well as "homes with front porches and a vibrant downtown where you'll see friends and neighbors," as its publicity brochure puts it. It promises all the accoutrements of the public square, the "building of a community," but Disney has prefabricated it along with instant "Celebration traditions" (a "fun-filled interactive orientation session"—a novel "tradition," to be sure!). Disney's traditions are no more traditional than its public squares are public. They are not born of blood, sweat, and tears—hard times and common experience forged over generations—but are "imagineered" by the same people who make the movies and create the rides and design the theme parks. In Celebration, lifelong community and permanent traditions are for sale today—public living without risk, diversity without tension, community without pain, tradition without history.

The true architecture of authentic public space is about diversity, and creating diversity is no easy architectural feat. Disney's style in Celebration has an archetainment feel to it—a Disney-clectic hodgepodge on the surface, with a comforting homogeneity lurking underneath. Like the Hollywood whose defining spirit and alter ego it has always been, Disney is necessarily parasitic: it creates nothing, living instead off other people's cultural capital. It homogenizes diversity just as it domesticates foreignness, contemporizes history, and privatizes public space. It gives you just enough history and culture and ethnicity and diversity to make sure you never have to deal with the real thing: the real public. Mexico without poverty or assassinations, Kashmir without altitude sickness or tribal war, Europe without foreign languages, France without snobbish waiters and people who think they're better than us, Germany without Dachau — community without hierarchy or clannishness, tradition without prejudice or inflexibility, friends without commitment or loyalty, public space for private use only, a town without pity or passion. Corporations like Disney imagine we have come to fear the very idea of real public space (space inhabited by the real, multicolored, multicultural public), and that makes the challenge of re-creating it particularly daunting.

Still, retrofitting commercial space as multi-use public space is a significant first step in giving our civil society a real geography. There are a few impressive examples: Mashapee Commons on Cape Cod or Ronald Sher's Crossroads in Seattle. But there are legal obstacles (many state courts have ruled that closed malls are wholly private), and there are political challenges: the danger of middle-class flight to private enclaves, for example, leaving "public" space to the poor, the unemployed, and the marginalized who are without the resources or tax base to create a usable commons of their own. Yet, without a commons, how are the poor, upon whom we heap new responsibilities in the era after big government, supposed to realize in practice the great ideals of civil society? Can reconstituted malls cut off from public transportation fulfill public purposes? These are the challenges.

THE NEW PUBLIC TELECOMMUNICATIONS
TECHNOLOGIES

As the world enters a new telecommunications and information age whose venue is cyberspace and whose viaduct is the informa-

tion superhighway, those of us who care about civil society must
have effective strategies to guarantee widespread public access and
broad civic usage. As the new technologies evolve, we must find
ways to counter wholesale commercialization of what Congress
defined as "public airwaves" and the new Internet conduits. Deregulation has focused on insulating productive market forces from
government intervention. President Clinton's policy paper released
in the summer of 1997 on "A Framework for Global Electronic
Commerce" made clear that, despite Vice President Gore's out-
spoken endorsement of the educational value of the new telecommunications technology, the Administration intends to expend
more energy fostering the private and commercial uses of the Net
than on its public and civic uses.* With the private sector focused
on profit and the government looking the other way, how can we
insulate civic and educational forces from the market in telecommunications?

There is a risk that those developing information technology will
focus either on national security (the Internet was born of Information Technology Warfare "ITW" research) or on profitable
commerce. Yet the rewarding civic domain, though profitless,
promises enormous potential benefits for democracy, civic culture,
and education. The challenge of a civic technology is particularly
important when government regulation and tax policy, the con-
ventional tools of the public good, are in such disrepute. Yet they
remain indispensable if the technology's civic is to be realized. The
World Bank offers an innovative model: it is examining the ways
in which technology can assist economic and civic development.
Satellite surveillance, for example, can aid agriculture by monitor-

---

*"A Framework for Global Electronic Commerce" offers government support for
common international technical standards, open access, privacy, and wholesale
commercialization, and suggests that the new technologies are to be viewed,
above all, as a vital component of world trade policy.

ing ecological change; cellular technology can allow areas still un-
wired for telephone to leapfrog over existing technologies and to
join the twenty-first century without even going through the twentieth. Since roughly half the globe is currently without phone service, this would be a striking development.[2]

It has been five years—an eon, these days—since Speaker Gingrich talked casually about providing laptops for Americans below
the poverty line. But to use computers, one must be user-literate,
and literacy is founded on lifelong education and an economy that
supports it, conditions that Gingrich did not address. Perhaps he
was merely posturing. More recently, President Clinton has endorsed an initiative (it is called Netdays) in which volunteers help
to hardwire inner-city schools with donated equipment. Demon-
stration projects like this are useful, but they are not the same thing
as a national policy, for if the Net becomes wholly commercial,
hard-wiring the schools is tantamount to commercializing them.
To avert this, an ongoing governmental effort is needed. The government need not and should not run programs that are platforms
for Net use or control the Net directly, but it can and should ensure
that commercial markets remain competitive, and that ample space
is left for local and regional public use, and it can and should fund
pilots so that we can inspect and try out various experimental civic
uses. For example, a civic chat-room facilitated by the League of
Women Voters or a publicly oriented electoral and political information site such as Project Vote-Smart or Minnesota E-Democracy
(nonprofit sites that try to make nonpartisan information available to
journalists and the public during elections).

The World Wide Web was, in its conception and compared to
traditional broadcast media, a remarkably promising means for
point-to-point lateral communication among citizens and for genuine interactivity (users not merely passively receiving information,
but participating in retrieving and creating it). But those who are
busy commercializing it are already moving away from the "pull"

programs that made the Net's early days interactive and participant-driven, and moving forward (backward!) to "push" programs, which look more like traditional advertising programming and pacify "clients" by using interactive information to anticipate ("guess") their interests and needs in order to sell them goods. Push technology wants to shape and guide your choices by inferring one want from another: if you logged on to the Boston Marathon's home page, you must like jogging, and if you like jogging, then you will probably want the latest Walkman. But if you spend your afternoons accessing films, you must be a couch potato, so here's a bargain on snack food, or, if it's film noir that's your passion, here's imitation art-deco jewelry.

There is nothing wrong with trying to make a profit by selling people what you guess they want, but when the Net becomes primarily or exclusively commercial, our capacity to choose is reduced to market appetites, and our potential for participation and interaction is reduced to rudimentary clientelism. In other words, without public intervention, the "new" Net technology becomes very much like the older technologies: passive, commercial, and monopolistic. First radio, then television, then cable were initially advanced as great new democratizing civic technologies in the public interest. Each in its turn grew into the commercial, privatized medium we know today, in which the public interest in civic culture, public education, and civil and political debate is marginalized and in which commercial selling and entertainment are front and center.

Government regulation, for which there is in any case little appetite, has not kept up with technological innovation. The Bill of Rights was written for a print world; the Federal Communications Act of 1934 was conceived for radio. The American government has yet to catch up to the implications of broadcast television, let alone of satellite and cable or fiber optics and computer chips. The public need for and civic use of these technologies have never been systematically contemplated. The government cannot and need not control them directly, but it has a fundamental responsibility to assure the American public and its civil-society institutions free and equal access and usage. Cyberspace is no less public than broadcast airwaves, and the information highway is a public, not private thoroughfare; it ought not to be commercialized and then sold back to its true owners, the American public.

We already face the irony that the "public airwaves" are leased by the government on behalf of the people to private commercial interests, which then sell them back to the American people for outrageous prices—corrupting the electoral process and making office-holding a privilege of the rich (or those willing to devote themselves to endless fund-raising). And we now face the added insult to our sovereignty of a government policy that simply donates the new digitalized broadcast spectra (roughly six new broadcast outlets for every television station now broadcasting) to current licensees, in what even Republican Presidential candidate Robert Dole labeled in 1996 the "giveaway of the century."

Paul Taylor, a former *Washington Post* journalist, has a project to persuade both broadcasters and politicians voluntarily to make prime-time television slots available for serious political expression and debate during election campaigns. It is one useful starting place, an excellent example of a voluntary civil-society strategy in this domain. It has been endorsed by President Clinton but is being resisted by the networks, which do not wish to pay the costs. Why not make compliance with the Taylor proposal a condition for commercial use of the new digitalized broadcast spectra? Or invite rivals to propose other civic uses of the new spectra, and ask current license-holders to match them or give up their licenses? Realists will of course point out that the extraordinarily powerful current license-holders, not just as a lobby but as corporations controlling public information and influencing public opinion, will not stand for such government tactics. But their power is, precisely, another reason we need the countervailing power of democratic government. The object is not to have government monopolize the airwaves or own the information highway; it is guarantee that no one else be allowed to do so. That is presumably why the U.S. Justice Department has finally challenged the Microsoft Corporation's habit of compelling hardware manufacturers to carry only Microsoft's Web browser if they want to carry Microsoft's Windows.

Another useful strategy would have government use education and humanities funding to offset the baleful encroachment of corporate advertisers and promoters on America's higher-education telecommunications research programs and public-school media classrooms. The market makes its inroads through incentives—let us call them bribes—to institutions that cannot afford computers or television sets or software. Inner-city public schools in nearly every state—schools that need innovative hardware and software—are currently being forced to bid for new equipment and satellite broadcasts by selling their pupils as forced audiences for commercials. This is the mind-corroding tactic used by the K-III Corporation's Channel One, originally Chris Whittle's blunt instrument for exploiting the need of poor schools for equipment they cannot afford; they now have their three minutes of Channel One's hard advertising and nine minutes of soft news in more than 12,000 classrooms in nearly every state in the Union. Surely, if broadcasters "deserve" free access to the new digitalized bands which they are getting from the government, our children deserve free and equal access to the new technologies out of which digital broadcasting grows. Public schools and public libraries must be the primary, not the tertiary, beneficiaries of the information revolution, and the only body that can make that happen is the federal government. Netdays are fine, but it will take more than volunteers or even hardwired schools to create a civic internet.

One powerful way to utilize the new technologies on behalf of civil society is to establish a "national civic forum," in which civil speech and reasonable political argument among geographically and economically dispersed communities becomes possible. Such a forum could pull together via satellite uplinks dozens of groups, each a meeting of several hundred citizens gathered in their own neighborhood, so that they might converse and deliberate with one another on two-way television hookups, as well as with some primary national forum to which they are all linked. Think of an ABC Nightline Town Meeting hooked up to a dozen sites where other meetings have been convened, with people talking within their own groups but also to other assemblies all across the nation, and to a national television audience. This big electronic town meeting linking up smaller regional meetings might well ameliorate the damage done by demagogic talk-radio shows and a commercially dominated electoral process. Such a deliberative form of satellite interactivity invites vigorous public participation but, by its very nature, it would demand tolerance, mutual respect, and independent rational argument. It would originate in local communities, but still offer a genuine national conversation. A civic forum such as this, funded by the federal government but administered independently (say, again, by an experienced nonprofit group such as the League of Women Voters), would take some of the organizational and financial responsibility for our electoral debates off the television media and give them an incentive to sponsor free time for candidates. Eventually it could support international dialogues linking NGOs and foundations in several nations in a single conversation.

A national civic forum has many attractive features for civil society. It facilitates horizontal conversation among citizens rather than the more usual vertical conversation typical of communication between citizens and elites. It offers ongoing deliberation rather than a single event (such as a debate between Presidential election candidates) and utilizes both traditional (television) and new (satellite and interactive) media. This kind of direct interaction among citizens is already the preferred mode of communication for many civil-society organizations such as American Health Decisions (a national health-education organization with multiple state sites), the Industrial Areas Foundation (founded decades ago by the progressive Saul Alinsky, a community-organization movement that teaches ordinary women and men from every walk of life to educate and empower themselves politically), the National Issues forums of the Kettering Foundation (which has organized hundreds of citizen groups around the country to reach consensual positions on fundamental policy issues), the Study Circles Movement (based on the Swedish practice of bringing together small groups of neighbors to discuss anything from fly-fishing to abortion policy, and supported in an active civic form today by the Topsfield Foundation), policy juries (that convene small groups of citizens who consider and deliver recommendations on tough policy questions), and so-called deliberative video town meetings (a project of Professor James Fishkin of the University of Texas, who, taking the idea of Theodore Becker and others, has pioneered prime-time televised gatherings of citizens who over several days discuss issues with experts and politicians and modify their opinions and prejudices as a result). These and other practical, ongoing experiments among citizens, who—without thinking of themselves as constituting a government or public authority—come together to express their common aspirations as well as their conflicting interests, suggest that a national civic forum is not just pie in the sky but would offer real nourishment for hungry citizens. The advantage it has over many local experiments already under way is that it extends the compass of interest and the membership of the participants by utilizing computer and Internet technology and thereby overcomes some of their special-interest parochialism.

The Committees of Correspondence created during the Revolutionary War by citizens who felt unrepresented were a remarkable example of civil-society politics. Men gathered together

informally in these committees, which, being neither governmental nor private, were the first independent civic entities in a
nation experimenting with autonomy, and in time they produced
trained citizens who had had a common experience of institution-
building. A little more than a century later, populists and progressives sent speakers and facilitators to "ride the circuit," bringing
together communities of dispersed rural people in gatherings
where the visitor was educator, political mobilizer, and conversation facilitator. Throughout the nineteenth century, New England
town meetings and rural groups like the Grange gave America's
new citizens forums that brought communities together around
larger regional issues, tying them to people elsewhere with shared
aspirations yet different experiences (urban workers and rural ten-
ant farmers, for example). But by the twentieth century, America's
pell-mell growth had rendered these forms of association less feasible—until now, with the advent of the new technologies. We
have yet to reckon with the consequences of low-frequency broadcasts, public-access cable channels, videoconference up- and down-
links, and private-sector satellite transmission, let alone with the
possibilities of digitalized broadcasting, fiber optics, and a world-
wide communications net. Panglossians exult, but technology has
usually mirrored rather than transformed the society that creates
it. Europe's emerging civic society in the Renaissance used gun-
powder to enhance burgeoning democratization, but its discoverers
in China used it to secure the hold of tyranny. The new telecommunications technologies certainly change the boundaries of our
lives, but whether this will help or hurt democracy and civil society
is not yet clear.

"Local" loses much of its limiting force with technologies in
which global *is* local, for example; but whether this merely inter-
nationalizes commerce and consumerism or opens doors to international civic cooperation depends on factors other than the
technology. An American civic forum (or French or Swiss or Eu-

ropean or sub-Saharan African forum) is technically feasible, but
its success will depend on political and cultural rather than technological factors. A national civic forum would push the technology in a democratic direction. As happens with New England's
Representative Town Meetings in communities too large to convene the entire citizenry (where delegates are chosen to meet on
behalf of the entire town population), civic-forum meetings might
develop cross-sectional national representation with a sampling of
"institutional" citizens from foundations, schools, voluntary associations, civic groups, and social movements. These delegates (and
the local assemblies hooked up by satellite) might even be chosen
by lot, as happened in many ancient Greek city-states. Sortition
(the lottery) assumes civic competence on the part of every player
in civil society, and in doing so helps to forge that competence. It
assumes that any group of players drawn from civil society's constituents is as likely as any other group to be able to work for
common goods and civic interests.

Some may object that a civic forum is redundant in a democratically governed nation where legislatures and representative assemblies already give civil society ear and voice. Surely democratic
government itself offers citizens opportunities for public voice and
social organization. In a well-ordered polity, it might actually do
this; according to democratic theory, it is certainly supposed to.
But America's political house is in a state of disorder, and so are
many other nations' houses. Citizens are deeply suspicious of the
professional political classes, cynical about government and, hence,
about democracy itself. Here again the Committees of Correspondence seem apt models, for they were fostered by British subjects
with quasi-colonial representative institutions of their own which,
however, they did not feel belonged to them. They were meant
to be a novel means of interaction—political but at the same
time (because the colonial "government" was the enemy) extra-
governmental. The aim in a modern democracy is not, of course,

to create an alternative or parallel government or even an alternative legislative forum, but to help citizens and their many voluntary civic institutions speak in a common voice both to the private sector and to the government. Rather than displacing government or market institutions, a national civic forum facilitated by the new technologies could reinvigorate them and prepare the way for the relegitimation of strong democratic government, allowing citizens to rediscover their civic competence.

The fact that the United States is so vast and decentralized, geographically and ethnographically if not economically, means that a civic forum is both more necessary and more difficult to create than it might be for a smaller nation (although Europe as an emerging transnational entity faces the same challenges). Necessary, because when economic and political power are concentrated and monopoly is the rule, democratic power must also be concentrated effectively to offer monopoly a countervailing force; harder because participation is easiest locally and hardest nationally. Participation is parochial, power cosmopolitan: how does one unite the two? Can technology facilitate perhaps a forum of civic interaction that will bridge space and unite a nation's, even a whole continent's, hyper-diversified fragments?

It was the vast scale and heterogeneity of modern mass societies that created the imperative for representative government in the first place; and it was representative government that, following the iron law of oligarchy, in time distanced citizens from their delegates and compromised its own legitimacy. The solution to the problem of mass society became, in time, the problem. Revitalizing a strong democratic civil society can circumvent the abuses of representation while at the same time refurbishing its legitimacy. A credible public voice gives citizens an alternative mode of expression and weans them from dependency on public-opinion polls and the media, permitting the better angels of their nature (usually muzzled in a privatized, cynical society) to speak freely, and re-

legitimizing democratic institutions that depend on their participation. Technology, properly used, can help give expression to this
credible public voice.

PRODUCTION IN THE GLOBAL ECONOMY

Like everything else in a privatizing society dominated by commerce, technology's possibilities are circumscribed by its ownership. Ironically, at the very moment in the history of the West
when the transformation of a traditional durable-goods industrial
society into a post-industrial information society has given a hand-
ful of vertically integrated media, entertainment, and information
conglomerates global influence over our thoughts, tastes, feelings,
and ideas — hence our lives — we have voluntarily abjured our democratic sovereign power to control them. Unlike the nineteenth-
century trusts in oil, steel, and railroads to which they are often
compared, the new telecommunications monoliths — Disney/ABC,
Time-Warner/CNN, the News Corporation/Fox, Bertelsmann, Via-
com/Paramount, and Microsoft — monopolize not natural resources and durable goods, muscles of an industrial society's
growing body, but pictures, information, and ideas, the sinews of
post-industrial society's soul. Can these private corporations be
made publicly responsible for the outcome they produce?

By law, corporations are of course themselves creatures and beneficiaries of the states they now assail: the limited-liability corporation and the trade policies under which it operates are all
products of government: the "private" corporation is, in fact, public, and at best a forgetful child of its true parents, at worst an
ingrate and parricide. As Hobbes made clear enough in his great
book on sovereign power, *Leviathan,* in the state of nature there
is neither "mine" nor "thine," neither private property nor contractual association, only the war of all against all, and the life of
man nasty, brutish, and short.

To attack what one derogates as the "social collectivism" of democratic institutions is a very convenient tactic for corporations celebrating a private-market collectivism all their own. Their kind of privatizing "individualism," which defines so much of our ideological politics today, disempowers American citizens just when they most need their commonalty to contain the corporate entities trying to control their lives. We are thankfully rid of the political totalitarianism of communist statism, but we seem largely oblivious to the subtler forms of economic totalism for which "free" markets are responsible.

Among the fundamental principles that California Governor Pete Wilson enunciated during his unsuccessful 1996 Presidential campaign was one averring that "individuals should be responsible and accountable for their actions" and that "we should value family as the foundation of our society." Responsibility has become the leading principle of the new minimal-government politics shared by Tories and Labor, Republicans and Democrats—a politics that asks high-school community-service volunteers, welfare mothers, and disemployed workers to shoulder the burdens of the economy and the community, and to stop expecting government to remedy every social ill. It is time to make the same demand of corporations and businesses. Responsibility and power go hand in hand: nothing has greater power today than a multinational corporation; no group has been left with less responsibility. Citizens and politicians worry about ethics, character, and family values in a modern, secular world. The firms whose products, marketing strategies, and commercialism are often deeply anti-family (in consequence if not intent) have a responsibility. Jobs are being exported, communities decimated, health, safety, and environmental standards protected by American or German or French law regularly circumvented in foreign markets. The firms which downsize, sell off, or close down subsidiaries they have taken over, or which flee abroad to profit from the absence of public regulation in other nations have a responsibility. As the boundaries separating information and entertainment are deliberately blurred, films and music deliberately infused with violence and misogyny, colleges and classrooms deliberately commercialized, the companies that have done these things and are the financial beneficiaries have a responsibility.

Business people sometimes try to claim that they are subservient to consumers and merely give people what they want. They protest that the market is the perfect instrument of liberty since it empowers individual consumers to determine what is produced and how it is priced simply by the power of their choices. So it is the consumers who are responsible! But this claim is little more than a useful fiction. The ancient capitalist economy, in which products were manufactured and sold to meet the demands of consumers who made their independently forged needs known through the marketplace, has long since disappeared. In its place is a postindustrial economy in which needs themselves are manufactured to meet the supply of producers who make their products "necessary" through promotion, "spin," packaging, advertising, and "scientific" marketing. The market today has reversed the polarities of demand and supply, so that producers strive to create a market for products that are not necessarily related to essential human needs at all. The corporations that do this have a serious responsibility for the kinds of need they create, the kinds of life-style they encourage, and the kinds of innovation they press.

There was a time in America's history when greater civic demands were placed on business. Throughout the nineteenth century, it was assumed that free enterprise was a key agent of citizenship-building and moral character. At its outset, Jefferson had lauded the democracy of yeoman farmers and free artisans; at its end, moralists still lauded the democracy of shopkeepers and entrepreneurial small businessmen. No wonder observers worried that the great trusts and cartels of the Gilded Age, and later the catalogue and chain stores like Sears and Montgomery Ward, were not only existential obstacles to fair trade but a clear and present danger to civic life as well — "contrary to the whole genius of the American people and American Government, which is local self-control of affairs," wrote Montaville Flowers in his *America Chained*.[3] Flowers worried that the new conglomerates would reduce workers from the "status of independence to that of hirelings under humiliating regulations, thus . . . lowering the spirit of communities and the nation."

The political philosopher Michael Sandel has convincingly demonstrated that, throughout the 1920s and 1930s, only part of the reaction to trusts and chains was really about monopoly. He cites Justice Louis Brandeis's dissent in *Liggett Company v. Lee* (1933), which overthrew Florida's tax on chain stores: Florida's "purpose may have been a broader and deeper one [than revenues]. They may have believed that the chain store, by furthering the concentration of wealth and of power and by promoting absentee ownership, is thwarting American ideals; that it is making impossible equality of opportunity; that it is converting independent tradesmen into clerks; and that it is sapping the resources, the vigor and the hope of the smaller cities and towns."[4]

In the same spirit, the clergyman Henry A. Stimson insisted that business was "a school of character second only to church."[5] What these moralists understood was that in a society in which business influences so many aspects of private and public life it bears a shared responsibility for the ethical and civic atmosphere. Following their logic, it seems apparent that Wal-Mart is no less a threat to turn the United States into that nation of "hirelings and clerks" alluded to by Brandeis and Sandel than was Sears, Roebuck. By the same token, Disney's entertainment and information services present an even greater risk of corruption by materialism, greediness, and passivity than the Standard Oil or Ford Motor Company. What Sandel calls "the political economy of citizenship" that "from Jefferson to the Knights of Labor" had "sought to form the moral and civic character" of the nation through the cultivation of "producers — as farmers, or artisans, or small businessmen and entrepreneurs" — is in danger of vanishing and, with it, the notion that corporations have a civic responsibility.

Justice Brandeis was prescient. He thought the new production-consumption mentality, severed from civic concerns, would breed a new kind of noncitizen: "Thoughtless or weak, he yields to the temptation of trifling immediate gain, and, selling his birthright for a mess of pottage, becomes himself an instrument of monopoly."[6] Trifling immediate gain and a mess of "pottage" have now become our era's high moral ambitions.

The new moralists who applaud the containment of government like to make vigorous civic demands on pregnant children and unemployed immigrants; they might more appropriately make them on Time-Warner and Microsoft. We rightly ask whether schools adequately provide for the moral education of children. We also have the right to ask whether Disneyland and MTV and the mall do the same.

What was true for shopkeepers and entrepreneurs surely holds for the multinationals. If in Brandeis's time absentee ownership and financier control presented a "grave danger to democracy,"[7] do not fax-paper merger-and-acquisition deals and international currency markets still more gravely endanger democracy today? Neither Brandeis nor his later advocates like Hubert Humphrey were anti-capitalist or anti-business. Rather, their point was and is to give business a good dose of genuine competition and consumers a fair playing field.[8]

The current crop of progressives are critical of business, but often cast their criticism in the language of capitalist efficiency. As Sandel is quick to notice, contemporary consumer affair critics like Ralph Nader and Mark Green appeal not to virtue but to consumer interests and "efficient" production and distribution. This inverts the progressive agenda and, ironically, turns the villains with whom the century started into the heroes with whom it is preparing to conclude:

> For progressives of old, the chains had been the villains, cut-throat competitors whose discounts would destroy the small, independent druggists and grocers and small businessmen on whom democracy depended. For modern progressives, the discounters have become the heroes, whose low prices enabled consumers to avoid paying the Bloomingdale's price.[9]

Civic responsibility, being a partnership between government, civil society, and the private market, necessarily depends on the active collaboration of political leaders, citizens, and business people. Executives have for too long suffered a kind of corporate schizophrenia in which they hived off and buried their civic identities—the small voices within that screamed "I cannot do that to my spouse, my children, my neighbors, my world!" even as their corporate hands signed orders doing exactly "that" to everyone, including their loved ones. Unless they want to live divided lives, they must accommodate their business to their human side.

It is not really so hard. The logic of the social contract enacts a set of mutual obligations among the parties who establish and benefit from democratic government. As citizens, whether of France, Germany, Russia or the United States, we have already covenanted to establish a free democratic government, although we seem to have forgotten its origin in our sovereign contract. But the wall between public and private sectors has insulated corporations and their personnel from civic responsibility and allowed this corporate schizophrenia to insulate their women and men, whether employers or employees, from their obligations as citizens. As Donella Meadows has observed, "every day decent people clear-cut forests, fish the oceans bare, spray toxins, bribe politicians, overcharge the government, take risks with the health of their workers or neighbors or customers, cheapen their products, pay people less than a living wage for a day's work, and fire their friends."[10] It is not, she adds, that businessmen "sit around plotting how to poison rivers or subvert democracy . . . (or) conspire to pollute"; it is just that as executives they seem unable to act as citizens. Quite the contrary: the very citizens who otherwise might see government as an ally have as corporate managers encouraged and participated in dismantling the strong state society and the democratic regulatory institutions that enforced civic standards on them. This gives them self-imposed responsibilities they might have avoided in a strong state society (and, in a well-ordered society, *should* have avoided). In an ideal world I would prefer to have democratic government enforce public standards and leave corporations to the business of productivity and profit-taking; in the world we actually live in, the predicate for reestablishing a robust civil society is a new civic compact that specifically obligates corporations. Here is a template:

A Corporate Civic Compact for Private Sector Citizens

Preamble. Recognizing that democratic government is an instrument of a free society and that its elected officers and representatives are but accountable trustees of those who elect them; and

that the primary responsibility for the civic health both of government and society thus belongs to the citizens and associations that constitute civil society and the private sector; and

that the productive economy requires a free-market private sector to flourish, while civil association requires a free civil-society sector to flourish; and

that civil society occupies a space between the governmental and private sectors that can be destroyed by bloat and aggressive expansion from either side; therefore,

We the free citizens of civil society and the corporate managers, producers, shareholders, and workers of the private sector, integrating our economic and civic identities and acknowledging our primary responsibility for democracy, do therefore freely obligate ourselves to the following principles:

1. We will respect the independence and noncommercial character of civil society and actively work to prevent the privatization or commercialization of its spaces—whether those spaces are educational (no advertising in or commercial exploitation of the classroom), religious (no commercialization of religious holidays), public broadcast (no charge for civic and political use of public airwaves), or environmental (protection of parks, waterways, and outer space* from advertising and commercialization).

2. We will support the civic diversification of public space and support the redevelopment of what have become exclusively commercial spaces such as malls and theme parks back into true public spaces, creating a balanced social environment in which production and consumption are complemented by the cultural, religious, educational, philanthropic, and political-social activities of civil society.

3. We will work to guarantee full public and equal access by every part of civil society to the media, traditional and innovative, broadcast and cable, passive and interactive, on which information, culture, democratic discussion, and productive capacity depend; and we will support information equality and combat a gap between the information-rich and the information-poor that destroys the conditions of political and civic equality on which democracy depends.

4. We will pay special attention to diversity and independence in the information and entertainment sectors where creativity, spontaneity, and innovation, which are indispensable to a free society, are cultivated and where the heterogeneity of

*The technology is available to put electronic billboards on satellites or Mickey Mouse ears on the moon.

information and debate that is the chief object of the Bill of Rights is secured.

5. We will treat employment not only as a function of economic efficiency and the profitability of production but as a fundamental social commitment, for work, whether commercial or civic, private or public, is the measure of human dignity and civic status, and social stability and labor morale depend on private, commercial, or civic work for all.

6. We will treat fair compensation and reasonable pension plans as rights that are indispensable to workers' dignity and status as citizens as well as their efficiency as producers and their power as consumers.

7. We will make a safe workplace and a safe environment the necessary conditions of doing business in a responsible manner that honors our owners, managers, and producers in their capacity as members of civil society.

8. We will encourage worker participation and worker shareholding through employee stock-ownership plans, codetermination, worker participation in management, and other forms of active worker engagement.

9. We will establish standards for safety, health, working hours, pension plans, and child-labor regulations that will be universally applicable, whether our facilities are located within or outside our company's headquarter nation; and we will pressure host foreign governments to accept and enforce these standards on all producers as a condition of our doing business in the host country.

10. We will establish standards for compensation that, while they may vary from country to country, offer a reasonable living wage by the measures of the host country; and we will pressure host governments to accept and enforce such standards on all producers as a condition of our doing business in the host country.

11. We will establish standards for compensation that link the salaries of all personnel to productivity, proportionally relate

increases in executive salaries to those in workers' wages, and maintain a differential ratio of lowest and highest salaries, whether stockboy or CEO, of no more than twenty to one (that's $20,000 for the clerk, $400,000 for the executive).

12. We will nourish diversity and competition and oppose monopolies, trusts, and cartels, not only because they restrict fair trade and capitalist innovation, but because they diminish the independence, liberty, and dignity of those who work for and manage them in ways destructive to civic virtue and democratic civic culture.

13. We will not take over or merge with other firms unless we intend to maintain their work forces; we will not use the sell-off or close-down of subsidiary companies to finance the takeover of parent companies; we will not engage in mergers and acquisitions whose only product is paper profits for buyers or sellers and the lawyers, accountants, and brokers who service them.

14. We will treat the placement of our facilities and plant in particular venues as a primary social and civic commitment and will not operate or uproot them without considering the social consequences for our employees and their communities, and without adequate compensation.

15. We will treat children and their education as special priorities of a free society, and will protect them from exploitation, from advertising that might distort their capacity for critical inquiry, and from products injurious to their health or polluting to their minds.

16. We will commit the resources necessary to execute the above obligations and treat them as a necessary cost of doing business in a democratic society, where executives and workers are citizens first and economic beings afterward.

17. We will spread the cost of this commitment of resources equally among all those who are social beneficiaries of social expenditures, including executives (modestly reduced sala-

ries), shareholders (modestly reduced profits), and customers
(modestly higher prices).

18. We will encourage personnel at all levels to overcome the
civic schizophrenia that forces us to regard ourselves as citizens in our social role but as corporate producers and managers in our economic role, and instead acknowledge that
our civic identity is primary and must play a primary role in
our economic decision-making.

I believe a commitment to this corporate civic compact will benefit the private sector no less than civil society. Rapacious capitalism
that brutalizes workers and rides roughshod over the common goods
of civil society in the long run only befouls its own nest. A free market undisciplined by civic concerns destroys citizens in the short
term but also destroys consumers in the long term. Henry Ford understood well enough that a living wage and a fully employed public
were conditions on which the selling of his cars depended. If his
workers couldn't buy his cars, to whom would he sell them? If "the
end of work," as Jeremy Rifkin has warned in his book of the same
title, is an unavoidable economic consequence of post-industrial
capitalism, then capitalism will have to look to something other than
pure economics for a guarantee of employment. Family values and
civic virtue are products of socialization, which means that the be-
hemoths ever more responsible for socialization will have to consider the moral and civic effects of their mind-bending software and
their durable products, and look to the social consequences of their
economic and fiscal policies. If they wish to indulge their self-
serving propensity to discipline and curtail government in the name
of free markets, free-market multinationals will have to discipline
themselves from within — or spin off into a self-destructive anarchy
of cartelism, gargantuanism, privatism, and disemployment that will
in effect knock the pegs out from under them as efficient economic
organizations. They have conspired in delegitimizing those who

once did their civic work for them, and in any case now operate in an international arena where there are no countervailing governmental institutions, so they now have to shoulder the burden themselves. Capitalism needs democracy and civility, which means it needs to democratize its practices and civilize its executives. Where once we looked appropriately to the sovereign polity to bring justice and comity to an otherwise anarchic economic realm, we must now also look to the newly sovereign corporations. Either they must give us back our government and, while pursuing profits, accommodate governmental encroachments and regulation in the name of the public weal, or they themselves will have to become more civic-minded and democratic, no matter what the cost to their profits. Anything less means the end of democracy.

CONSUMPTION IN THE GLOBAL ECONOMY

We can demand from corporations greater civic responsibility, but we do not have to await a new corporate spirit in order to counter the current irresponsibility. We can do plenty of things on the consumer side to nurture greater corporate virtue, using a civil-society strategy to form "civic consumers cooperatives" aimed at changing corporate behavior.

Once upon a time, the goods Americans purchased were unknown entities, safe or unsafe, clean or polluted—there was no way for us to know. In time, the safety of goods was assured by government-imposed standards. But the ideology that made regulation of this kind politically viable is no longer popular and the globalization of markets, which has permitted corporations to flee the control of sovereign national governments and set up production facilities in countries where reasonable standards may not exist, has created problems for consumers and for American workers—whose high wages in part reflect the high standards of American-produced goods.

A civil-society approach to solving this problem would enhance corporate responsibility by using the demand side, the consumer side, to modify corporate behavior. This strategy borrows from traditional voluntarist tactics of the kind used in, say, the "union label" approach, or the *Good Housekeeping* "Seal of Approval," or the Underwriters' Laboratory (U.L.) label for safely wired electrical products, or the Consumers' Union's testing and branding of goods for safety, quality, and plausible pricing. The same approach has been used more recently in the international domain by the Rugmark program, originating in Germany (a large importer of rugs), which identifies rugs that are made without child labor, and the Dolphin Safe Tuna program, which induces tuna fishermen to avoid the netting practices that kill dolphins. After a great deal of adverse publicity (Kathy Lee Gifford with her Wal-Mart line and Michael Jordan with his Air Jordan shoes for Nike were both assailed for representing companies that violated American standards), the clothing industry is also moving in this direction with its Apparel Industry Partnership. These positive strategies are an affirmative version of another, better known but less effective one — the boycott. Boycotts, however, have a punitive aspect and can be offset by counterboycotts: a company like Disney can as easily be boycotted by gays for honoring Baptist anti-gay sentiments as by Baptists for pro-gay employment benefit practices. Trade boycotts also risk being declared illegal internationally where free trade agreements reign. (The World Trade Organization had declared consumer boycotts incompatible with membership!)

The idea of a civic consumer coalition is intended not to punish "bad" producers but to reward "good" ones. To work, programs like Rugmark and the Apparel Industry Partnership need strong public support. The premise is that consumers, while primarily concerned with variety, quality, ease of purchase, and (above all) price of goods, also care enough about civic and social values to include them as part of their calculation about which goods (or which brand of goods) to buy. A significant proportion of consumers prefer to buy goods and brands that are produced without child labor, unfair employment practices, or indecent wages (as measured in-country), and without endangering workplace safety or the environment—especially when the goods are made in countries where American or European standards do not prevail by corporations that went to those countries precisely to increase profits and lower costs. We might say that civilized (civil) consumers want good-quality products at a good price which are also *child-labor safe, fair-wage safe, workplace safe, and environmentally safe.*

Firms that produce such goods and can verify that they do so with trustworthy (external) inspection and certification*—a "Safe" label, say, certifying the four safe categories—would have a clear marketplace advantage, even if their prices were marginally higher. Indeed, the added volume of sales might enable them to keep prices down. This demand-side market approach, it should be emphasized once again, does not punish corporations that disregard the civic-consumer rules, but it does benefit the civic-minded corporations that do play by the rules.

Once upon a time, a label announcing "Made in America" or "union made" gave products a trade advantage. Today, a CCC (Civic Consumers Coalition) SAFE label would enable consumers to offer producers powerful economic incentives voluntarily to meet "American" safety standards in these four domains, no matter where their facilities are located. Such a label, incorporating Rugmark and the "No Sweat" benchmarks, would provide a universal standard recognized around the world. The burden would be shifted from negative control via regulation of production to positive control via consumer oversight. At the same time, firms that stayed at home and

*The Belgrade Manual of Rules of the International Law Association stipulates all human-rights inspections must be made by independent experts, not by those being inspected.

met the already high government and state standards that prevail in the United States and Europe would find their higher-priced goods and higher production costs competitive after all, since the foreign-made goods would eventually bear some of the same costs. Companies would have less incentive to leave home in the first place, and those that did would no longer be rewarded for recklessness and irresponsibility.

A civic consumer cooperative would also help consumers to formulate their economic decisions as civic decisions, with the social consequences now calculated as part of a product's cost. How much would civic consumers pay for the label? The market itself would answer the question, though surveys suggest declining consumer cooperation when prices rise more than five or ten percent. Traditionally, the civic purpose of public decision-making and the commercial function of private decision-making were separated, and properly so, with government carrying the main burden. As early as 1930, Congress passed a law prohibiting the import of goods manufactured with the participation of forced or indentured labor (convict labor, for example), and a bill is currently pending that would extend that prohibition to goods made with child labor, a bill which if passed would represent "an incredible breakthrough" in curbing the abuse of children around the world, as one journalist has put it.[11] Whether or not this bill becomes law (and there are inevitable questions about its compatibility with the World Trade Organization's insistence that governments remain laissez-faire with respect to such issues), in this era of political skepticism and animus against regulations, the responsibilities once shouldered by government must be taken on by producers and consumers. And since producers are not likely to do their part without prompting from consumers, consumers must learn to think like citizens, bringing their private choices into line with their public responsibilities. A Civic Consumers Coalition with the means to influence producers becomes a new and powerful tool of the public good, another way to take civil society seriously.

As I have noted, consumer pressure, celebrity embarrassment, and pressure from the political side have already offered an immediate test of the idea of a civic consumers cooperative in one specific sector: the apparel industry. The Workplace Code of Conduct agreed to in the spring of 1997 by a Presidential task force (jawboned into being by President Clinton under the inviting title Apparel Industry Partnership and including not only Liz Claiborne and Nike but other major manufacturers such as Reebok and Nicole Miller) prohibits signatories to the code from using forced labor and young children, and requires companies and their contractors to pay the minimum wage as stipulated by local law, and to abide by other safe workplace standards.[12] The signatories' "No Sweat" logos on their labels will alert consumers to the salutary conditions under which their products were manufactured. In this case, we are actually on the verge of doing something effective to control a supposedly uncontrollable international market.

CIVIC EDUCATION
AND COMMUNITY SERVICE

The fostering of national and community service programs has been one of the Clinton Administration's great bipartisan success stories, yet it has come under fire from the congressional Republicans and seems forever at risk. Still, the Administration has been firm in treating service as a crucial attribute of citizenship and an activity of civil society rather than as a "government program," and this could go a long way to securing its future in America. After all, what is more civic than community service? But because the Clinton program was seen in some quarters as either an attempt to mandate voluntarism (it was not) or a device to find a new basis for a school-loan program (which it was only secondarily), it became a target of partisan wrangling. Congress tends to focus on "outcomes" and effectiveness (how many meals dispersed to homeless people? how many hours spent tutoring? how many senior shut-ins assisted?), and while this may be politically useful, it diverts attention from the primary goal: to teach social responsibility and citizenship to those doing the service. Underlining the learning dimension, and gaining a better sense of how these service programs promote civic education, can lower the "outcome" expectations and earn more credit for the good public work the programs actually do—to and for volunteers and the communities they serve—and not just in the near term.

An important first step has been taken by the Partnering Initiative on Education and Civil Society, a ten-year program launched by the Department of Education, the National Association of Education, and important public and private education groups.[13] By putting civic education on a par with other basic school skills, this initiative repositions education as critical for citizenship. A number of states, most notably Maryland, under the leadership of Lieutenant Governor Kathleen Kennedy Townsend (who was an advocate of school-based service long before her election), have introduced mandatory high-school community-service programs that are closely linked to classroom learning.[14] Putting service in the context of civil society and treating it as a concomitant of education makes it the first step toward lifelong citizenship, not just a temporary job that buys the government some social benefits in return for a wage measured in scholarship dollars.

Civil society depends on members serving what Alexis de Toqueville aptly called the arduous apprenticeship of liberty. We must learn to discuss public schooling, pedagogical standards, and federal money for education in terms of this crucial civic dimension. One of the most important original justifications for public and common schools was democracy's need for its young people to be educated, cognitively and behaviorally, as competent citizens. We do more nowadays to educate immigrants as citizens than we do to teach our own native-born Americans.

The federal government, through the Department of Education, can model civic curricula and service learning programs without spending large sums of money. The Department of Education might, indeed, strengthen its own case by focusing on this civic dimension, where its function as a national standard-setter is paramount. "Standards" might be more relevant if they included civic competence along with literacy and numeracy. By the same token, the volunteer effort on behalf of America's children, launched by General Colin Powell at the Presidents' Summit on America's Future in 1997, might better sustain civic and private momentum if it were more closely tied to the education of volunteers as well as to the education of those whom volunteers, through their service, educate in turn.

The partnership of government and civil society in fostering community service makes particular sense today, given the widespread popularity of education-based service programs in America's high schools and colleges. Community service was once an isolated Saturday afternoon extracurricular activity, but now it is recognized as a crucial component of a responsible academic curriculum that accepts schools as parts of their communities and that treats students as prospective citizens whose education must include civic competence. In recent years, to take just one example, the Ford Foundation has worked closely with the United Negro College Fund to nurture the development of education-based service learning programs in a dozen or more historically black institutions. Modest philanthropic dollars and robust outside guidance have allowed the colleges to build good programs without becoming dependent on external resources. A modest government program on this model, supporting a partnership with community organizations, colleges, and the non-profit sector, could accomplish a great deal without breeding dependency or overburdening taxpayers.

The European Commission has done its own experimentation

with a European volunteer service program, presumably in the hope that service on this scale might help foster a more genuine sense of European citizenship.

The relationship of art and the humanities to a free democratic society, to its diversity and pluralism, its manifold liberties, its openness and flexibility is complex and often problematical. The arts can flourish in democracy, but it is also true that they have often developed with remarkable vibrancy in autocratic societies as well as in cultures of dissent or rebellion. Still, democracy needs the arts and the humanities, since they constitute the cultural infrastructure of civil society. Yet the democratic impulse has sometimes been at odds with art and been threatened by avant-garde or anti-majoritarian or aristocratic cultures.

So democracy perhaps needs the arts more than the arts need democracy—although the symbiosis between the two is obvious and vital in a functioning free society. For a free society affirms its liberty and democratic vitality in civil society, and the arts and humanities invest that civil society with its creativity, its diversity and liberating spontaneity. What complicates the relationship is the market, which offers space to art and culture that insulates them from governmental direction and censorship. Yet because market space is also commercial space, commerce and exchange can imperil the autonomy of the arts.

Art and culture are, to be sure, resilient. Without subsidy, even without democracy, and under the conformist pressures of political autocracy or majoritarian mass opinion, the arts have survived. They are rooted in indelible human genius and an irrepressible need for authentic self-expression and communication, which surface under—indeed, sometimes are catalyzed by—the most repressive imaginable conditions, including the Gulag and the extermination camp. They are as difficult to root out and destroy as the human spirit itself. We were never so free, said Jean Paul Sartre, as during the Nazi Occupation.

But this durability of art is not an adequate reason to avoid asking the hard questions about arts policy in a democracy. After all, democracy and the arts share common roots in their common relationship to a robust civil society. As John Dewey noted, democracy is as much a way of life as a form of government, and its success depends on the existence of a vigorous civil society.

The arts are civil society's driving engine, the key to its creativity, its diversity, its imagination, and hence its spontaneity and liberty. As democracy depends on civil society for its liberal spirit, so civil society depends on the arts; thus democracy needs the arts' commitment to free creativity, liberal diversity, and unfettered imagination. A government that supports the arts is not engaging in philanthropic activity but assuring the conditions of its own flourishing. This is perhaps the most important single argument in favor of a democratic government caring about and nurturing the arts: not because the arts need it, but because democracy needs the arts. Europe has learned this lesson.

Under normal circumstances, the arts can survive without democratic support—indeed, without a democratic constitution—however much a democratic way of life needs their creativity and critical imagination, however much it is enhanced by a robust civic infrastructure nourished by art. Our circumstances today in the United States are not entirely normal, however. Under the adverse conditions of pervasive mass commerce, and given our growing ambivalence about diversity and pluralism, the arts may both be at risk and be necessary in unprecedented ways. Consequently, there are new arguments to make in favor of a modest government commitment to arts education, and for incentives and subsidies for creation and performance in the overweening commercial environment, and our ever more diversified and (some fear) fragmented society.

Art today has more to fear from the uncoerced, largely invisible constraints of commercialization than it does from pushy or censorious governments. Although artists certainly have the "right" to isolate themselves from society and pursue their muses free of interference, they may discover that by taking on responsibilities for arts education and civic engagement they contribute to a climate from which they benefit. Artists as artists are responsible only to their art, but artists are also citizens, and as citizens they have a particular responsibility: in contributing to and nourishing an arts-supportive civil society, they serve both democracy and themselves, both their fellow citizens and their art.

Advocates of laissez-faire privatizing, suspicious of government meddling in the arts, may believe that they are supporting a merely private (and liberal) domain. But when civil society is collapsed into the commercial market sector, as has happened today, privatization means commercialization, and the arts are subjected to the harsh interventionist dynamics of commerce. Neither high art nor rebellious art nor even ordinary amateur art (community theater, for example) can thrive under such conditions. The market pushes toward a uniformity of taste, a leveling of standards, and radical commodification. Yet "art products" satisfy almost no one. Magazines trump books, newspapers trump magazines, tabloids trump newspapers, television trumps tabloids, MTV trumps television — until not even popular culture in its full diversity can survive, let alone anything else.

When the market for arts, "free" in theory, is in practice often monopolistic in ownership and comformist in taste, not just high art and rebellious art but popular culture, too, needs the incentives and balancing support of government and arts-council subsidy. "Public" television in America has offered a place on the broadcast spectra where "other" tastes — some "high," some "popular," but in any case not likely to flourish in a pure market environment — can educate, cultivate, and entertain audiences. Why should so modest a presence, for so modest a cost, be seen as a harbinger of government-sponsored taste or a usurpation of an otherwise quite nearly sovereign set of commercial market mechanisms and commercially uniform values?

Ours is not only a democratic market society but also a pluralistic society that has recently become so diversified and differentiated that historians have begun to worry about the disintegration of our cultural fabric. (Arthur Schlesinger, Jr., made this point in his *The Disuniting of Democracy*, for example.) In this regard, we must remember that the arts can simultaneously express the particular identities of communities and groups (including those that feel excluded from the dominant community) *and* capture universalities that bring distinctive local communities together in a national whole. The Southern novel did not fragment America: it helped to define an American perspective. The Hudson River School of painters represented an emerging American taste in the nineteenth century, just as New England transcendentalism helped to create an American philosophical perspective. Jewish culture in New York helps to tie the city together even as it gives special expression to a particular identity. In music and theater, American blacks have stamped our national culture with many of its best-known American themes. Jazz, tap, blues, and the broader popular music culture of which they are a part at once define America and define one special contribution of African-Americans to it. This power to give voice to, hence to empower and recognize, marginalized and minority cultures, and at the same moment to constitute them as an inclusive common culture from which none is excluded, is unique to the arts.

Imagination is the link to civil society that art and democracy share. When imagination flourishes in the arts, democracy benefits. When it flourishes in a democracy, the arts and the civil society the arts help to ground also benefit. Imagination is the key to diversity, to civic compassion, and to commonalty. It is the faculty by which we stretch ourselves to include others, expand the compass of our interests, and overcome the limits of our parochial selves. Only then do we become fit subjects to live in democratic communities. The democratic citizen needs critical imagination to ward off tyranny and defend liberty. The artist needs critical imagination to ward off convention and defend creation. Even where the arts defy convention, outrage taste, and flaunt democratic mores, democracy needs them. It is only a mature democracy that fully appreciates these links. Ironically, youthful democracies, which most need the arts to grow and mature, are least likely to have governments that support art. It has been a mark of America's maturity as a free society that it has become less fearful of the positive European model, and has sustained the arts without becoming either proprietary or censorious.

To be sure, art will not perish in the absence of active support and understanding from a democratic people and their government. Nor will democracy wilt and die in the absence of a robust arts policy and a vibrant arts community. But democracy will do better, and the arts will do better, when democratic citizens and their governments support them. Democracy has most to gain by cultivating and supporting artists and the arts. Though they remain stubborn, independent, cranky, rebellious, sometimes ungrateful, and always subversive, our artists cultivate and manifest the liberty that lies at the very core of democracy's liberal soul.

These six examples of practical approaches to reestablishing civil society (or, where it survives, reinvigorating it) argue for social realism, for a strong democratic vision of civil society in which citizens occupy an independent space between government and the private sector. They demonstrate that civil society is far from being an esoteric normative ideal or a remote subject of nostalgic memory or, worse yet, some social-science construct invented by scholars to let them play self-righteous scold to wayward citizens. On the contrary, it has vital political and civic importance in defining legislative and corporate strategies that can make society both more civil and more democratic. The theory of civil society has a potential practice that is realistic and pragmatic — and hence transpartisan but also progressive.

Yet the six areas portrayed here as ripe for legislative action and government/civil society partnerships do not address two troubling questions raised by the weakness of modern civil society: the growing incivility of our political discourse; and, in an ever more automated workplace, the continued hiving off of wage-earning work from every other kind of public work and activity (including leisure activity), which has left labor markets roiling and created such frustrating anomalies as a welfare strategy intent on evicting mothers from their deeply consequential "jobs" raising children and maintaining a home life alleged to be indispensable to family values and civic virtue, in the name of securing them inconsequential "real jobs" in a commercial sector whose long-term problem is an absence of meaningful employment. These two sets of challenges cannot be addressed by developing simple government/civil society partnerships. They pose basic dilemmas regarding the meaning of civility and the future of work in societies trying to mobilize their dormant civic realms and energize their citizen resources in what is a promising but daunting age of advances in telecommunications technology, downsizing of labor forces, and globalization of markets. In the last two chapters, I address these dilemmas.

4

CIVILITY AND CIVILIZING DISCOURSE

Civil society is a domain of talk, civil talk.[1] In restoring the health of civil society, we also restore the civility of discourse, and in rendering our political and private talk more civil, we can repair our civil society.

Civility is, precisely, civil society's contribution to our political conversation. Giving a civic public voice legitimate civil articulation is a priority for all of us who want to invest that once sublime title *citizen* with renewed meaning. "Civil" is a vitally important prefix: it modifies "disobedience" as well as "society," and points to an other-regarding, undogmatic tolerance in confronting the political conflict that is essential to democracy.

Usually, the meaning of terms like "civil" and "public" is left indeterminate, hostage to enthusiastic but ultimately vacant rhetoric. Indeed, civility comes too often to mean simply docility or tranquillity. The 1996 Presidential debates were in this sense civil to a fault—excruciatingly civil in the eyes of noisy traditionalists hoping for a "horse race" (they usually mean a "hoarse race"). Yet civil resistance is hardly docile, and deliberative discourse is neither conflict-avoiding nor soporific, though it may be something less than riveting entertainment. Unfortunately, in a commercial society, entertainment trumps information, which is why broadcasters so resist the idea of affording the public "free" time for political debate and argument. Bad enough that they cannot sell ads to sponsor such civic activity; what if nobody watches? if viewers flee to the competition?

Civil talk is in the first instance public talk, but making talk public is not automatically to civilize it. Talk radio is loudly public without being in the least civil, though it is seductively entertaining. Unfortunately, its divisive rant is a perfect model of everything that civility is *not*: people talking without listening, confirming dogmas, not questioning them, convicting rather than convincing adversaries, passing along responsibility to others for everything that has gone wrong. And much of what passes for journalism, especially on television, is mere titillation or dressed-up gossip or polite prejudice. Because the pages of history devoted to peace are mostly blank, as Hegel reminded us, the preferred model for our public talk is war. A thoughtful and civil on-screen conversation I once had during the Reagan Administration with Chester Finn, Jr., then Undersecretary of Education, concluded with a plea from our producer that we reshoot the debate, this time with "more agitation and hostility, please." We complied with the director's request, but our adversarial reshoot pushed us away from common ground and from the provisional understanding we had achieved through an appreciation of our differences. The simulated "conflict" — more prosaic, less truthful, and much less productive — made for "better television." The reshoot, naturally, was the version that was eventually broadcast. And this on *public* television.

Opinion-makers who yell at one another on tele-tabloid shows like *Crossfire* and *The McLaughlin Group* demonstrate how long a journey it may be for women and men nurtured in the private sector to find their way to civil speech in its measured public voice.

Many mistake private-sector adversarial rants for acknowledgments of differences and thus for public talk. George Will ridiculed the idea of a national conversation on the meanings of America favored by Sheldon Hackney. The chairman of the National Endowment for the Humanities had made it the centerpiece of his tenure. Will suggested that the tele-tabloid talk shows proved we are *already* holding plenty of conversations. But whatever else they may be— demagoguery, commerce, entertainment, politics—these media happenings are not civic conversations but their precise contrary. When they start to be genuinely civic, they risk losing their audience. To hold viewers, they remain stubbornly unedifying, concealing honorable differences by harping on dishonorable squabbling. The Clinton "scandals" are more of the same.

We need then to grapple with this public ambivalence about civil deliberation. As with government services, for which citizens clamor even as they refuse to pay the taxes that provide them, so with civility—it's something we want for free, not wanting to pay its civic costs. We demand it in theory and avoid it in practice. We watch the scandal mongering we deplore, and civility slips away.

Among the characteristics which render talk genuinely public and civil (and which are missing in media talk) are the following, though, to be sure, they are in some tension with one another:

Commonalty. A public voice expressing the civility of a coop- erative civil society speaks in terms that reveal and elicit common grounds, cooperative strategies, overlapping interests, and a sense of the public weal. This means it is more than simply an aggregate of private voices, yet it cannot be an external (heteronomous) voice imposed on citizens who have not participated in constructing it. A common voice is shared by individuals as individuals (and thus expresses their interests) but denotes something they have in com- mon (what defines them as a community).

Deliberation. The public voice of civility is deliberative, critically reflective as well as self-reflexive; it can withstand reiteration, critical cross-examination, and the test of time. This guarantees a certain distance, a certain dispassion and provisionality. It is also dialectical, transcending contraries without surrendering their distinctions, just as a good marriage between strong individual partners makes them one without undermining their "two-ness."

Inclusiveness. Civility's public voice is inclusive: outreaching and multi-vocal. This may seem to contradict the need for commonalty, but rather than denying difference, democratic commonalty acknowledges and incorporates it; it seeks what is shared, rather than suborning the individual in some putatively trans-individual or holistic community. Commonalty is easily secured by exclusion, but at the cost of freedom and equality. To remain democratic, multivocality and its twin, dissent, must be voiced: this is the real test of inclusiveness. A public voice is a microphone for people on the margins, people disempowered by the hegemonies of government and the monopolies of the private sector. Debates in the private sector are clublike: discretionary, self-selecting, subject to exclusion. Despite the noisy dissension on shows like *Crossfire*, the real dissidents and the silenced minorities are rarely heard on them. And debates within government, while technically open to all, are too often professional and technocratic and thus in their own way closed. To be part of the voice of civil society is a right and an obligation and thus should be denied to no one. Inclusiveness has costs: it can foment anarchy. To achieve multivocality without cacophony is a high art, and it calls for special civic practices. Common talk that excludes is clear but undemocratic, and it endangers people. Talk that is too inclusive results in babble, democratic but perilous to community.

Provisionality. Because an open and inclusive public is itself an evolving political entity, the public voice is always provisional, subject to emendation, evolution, and even contradiction. The closure that comes with almost every exclamation on talk radio — a caller cut off, squelched, disconnected — is perhaps its most uncivil feature. True public dialogue is ongoing and has no terminus, only a series of provisional resting points where action becomes possible prior to further debate. This is perhaps why Jefferson recommended a little revolution every nineteen or twenty years. He suggested that principles we have not embraced as our own, generation by generation, lose their legitimacy, however constitutional their origin and however just their substance.[2] This feature of the public voice immunizes it against dogmatism and expresses democracy's tolerant, open-minded spirit. It explains why no public can be bound by its predecessors or can bind its successors, and why each generation must express its own faith in constitutional democracy all over again.

Listening. The public has not only a voice but an ear: the skills of listening are as important as the skills of talking. Private interests can be identified and articulated simply by *speaking* authentically out of one's own needs and wants. Public interests can be identified and articulated only when people *listen* to one another, only when they modulate their own voices so that the voices of others can be heard, assimilated, and accommodated if not fully harmonized. Listening is civility's particular virtue. If government opts for "parliaments" (from *parler*, to talk) where talking and the differential skills it exhibits are privileged, the civic forum demands an "audioment" where the more egalitarian skills of listening are nurtured. Like Quakers, citizens ought not to fear silence in their civil assemblies. Only when the articulate are silent are the weak uncertain voices of the inarticulate and powerless likely to join the conversation and be heard. Listening thus becomes a powerful guarantor of inclusiveness.

Learning. The public voice requires a public ear, and, similarly, to participate in civil talk is necessarily to be open to learning—listening's most sublime fruit, which makes us able to question opinions we formerly held and change positions we formerly took. When talk is merely an exchange of fixed opinions and politics is a series of compromises in which positions are arbitrated but never altered, then citizenship is impaired. Imagine a *Crossfire* in which one pigheaded pundit declared to another: "I hadn't thought of that! Yes, perhaps I need to review my ideas and reposition myself. I won't comment further until I have really absorbed and thought through what you just said." Imagine a squawk radio host confessing to a listener: "I think I understand you better now. I want to take a few days to think about what you've said; I may just have to change my mind." Unimaginable? Probably. Yet talk that polarizes is based on the idea that people are citizens only inasmuch as they are defined by immutable, irreducible interests, and that conversation can do little more than give them a chance to articulate and adjudicate those interests. Learning, on the other hand, presumes that opinion is mutable and that viewpoints can be modified and can grow. "It is actually in my own interest to include your well-being," says the civil speaker who through conversation with an "adversary" has discovered common ground.

Lateral communication. The dialogue between government and voters is most often dyadic and vertical: a two-way conversation between elites and followers, where leaders talk at their constituents and occasionally are talked *to* by them. But a public voice leads to a multivocal *lateral* conversation *among* citizens rather than between them and their "leaders." The dyad is replaced by the community—embodying not a single integral point of view but an evolving collection of intersecting, overlapping viewpoints. As we have noticed, the clearest sign of the eclipse of civil society has been the disappearance of those nongovernmental spaces where citizens can talk to one another—the barbershop, the public square, the community hall, the general store, the schoolyard, the public library—what Harry Boyte calls our "free spaces" where we can talk with and listen to one another.[3] The highway, the drive-in, the fast-food emporium, and the mall are public without being civic. The few public institutions left to us are underfunded, overwhelmed, and under siege. We have seen that public schools and universities are compelled to sell themselves in the private sector — turning over classrooms to commercial sponsors (like Channel One) in order to get desperately needed electronic hardware, to write single-vendor contracts with corporations that promise them millions of dollars in return for exclusive sales rights and a piece of the university's good name. Churches, too, accommodate themselves to privatization and become instruments of a divisive, extremist politics and of demagogic leaders, rather than of ecumenical integration and communication among parishioners and between congregations. The media, subordinated to commerce and thus privatized, sell gossip and scandal and instant opinion rather than offering an information window on the public world.

A certain kind of log-rolling politics ("You'll get yours if I get mine") can come from vertical elite-mass conversation, but a true public voice emerges only from lateral conversation. In the absence of appropriate arenas, the civic forum must create its own geography.

Imagination. The civility of public voice is impossible in the absence of imagination, which counts as the single most important mark of the effective citizen. Through imagination, private interests are stretched and enlarged to encompass the interests of others, while the wants and needs of others can be seen to resemble our own, and the welfare of our extended communities can be recognized as the condition for the flourishing of our own interests. What is a bigot other than a man without imagination? a woman unable to see beyond her own color or religion into the kindred soul of a being different but the same? The public voice is one of a private self empathizing with the interests of others not as an act of altruism but as a consequence of self-interest imaginatively reconstructed as common interest. It is not an accident that theorists as diverse as Hume and Rousseau considered imagination and empathy to be the key to humankind's social skills.

Empowerment. Public talk capacitates; civility empowers. Talk that is civil is shared talk and is the basis for shared action, turning talkers into doers. Rights secure our negative liberty, but since they are often claimed against others, they entail being left alone. In their laissez-faire form, they can mandate inaction. Responsibilities, on the other hand, involve us with others and entail action. If Jack and Jill have a responsibility to Héloïse and Abelard, they must not just feel but must *do* for Héloïse and Abelard. Talk that does not foresee action and look forward to consequences is just a game or a pleasant pastime or an intellectual exercise. Talk-show rhetoric can afford outrage and excess, precisely because it is inconsequential: nothing is really at stake. Talk aimed at common work and actions disciplines itself, and pulls back from excess. This moderation empowers the talker to collaborate and deal with conflict, to solve problems, to secure common goals. And since civil talk is provisional (that being one of its strengths, as we have seen), civil action is marked by moments of rest and a temporary suspension of debate, when decisive action becomes possible. Thus the "public" in public talk looks to a world of action where consequences count—in sharp contrast to private talk, where nothing common is at stake and where arguments may be pursued endlessly since nothing public turns on their outcome (or even on their having an outcome). Since true public talk results in public action, a failure to reach a decision (a non-decision) is itself a kind of action with its own public consequences.

The embeddedness of civic talk in action raises a troubling dilemma for public talk: Why is it that even when this model of civility is understood, it is not more popular? Media talk is divorced from action, and its irresponsibility feeds its incivility. Journalists tell, they don't do. News is entertainment, a commodity, not a sine qua non of a free society. Journalists sell advertising rather than papers, television spots rather than television news. When Rush Limbaugh cites unnamed sources that charge President Clinton

with murder, it's all just talk—funning and fuming to pump up
the ratings on which the price of spot commercials is based. But
a grand-jury indictment on charges of homicide is a very different
matter. A motion to impeach is the gravest one the United States
Congress can make, while an aside on talk radio accusing a President of infidelity or treason is just an attention-grabber.

Talk concerning action—news about politics—should be
responsible precisely because it has consequences, just as politics
does. Civility is not about politeness; it is about responsibility,
which is why disobedience can also be civil. Public talk is civil
society's special form of power: it sets the agenda for common
action and provides the language by which a community can pursue its goods—or assail an irresponsible government or even indict
its own failure to pursue goods. Whether it empowers is hence a
crucial test of whether talk is genuinely public, just as whether it
is civil is a crucial test of whether it is responsible. Civility confronts brute force with reason. It distinguishes democracy (the politics of reason) from tyranny (the politics of force). Incivility is not
a rude form of political discourse, but a polite form of political
violence. When we cultivate truly civil media that respect reason
in a civil society, our politics become not conflict-free but responsible and empowering.

A public, civil voice is inflected very differently than either the
official, univocal voice of government or the obsessively contrary,
frequently uncivil talk of the private sector's multiple special interests. Inasmuch as it is marked by the quest for commonalty
despite honest differences, for responsibility despite antagonism, for
recognition of the other despite divergent self-interests, it is not just
about the tenor or tone of our politics but about its very substance.

The nine characteristics of civil talk that I have enumerated are
clearly normative and can be realized in practice only when institutions foster them, and only when we citizens take a more consistent approach to politics. We have to decide whether we want

bread, circuses, and horse races from our politics, or the conditions—not always so entertaining—that make possible civil self-government and long-term democracy.

Here is the real challenge to democratic proponents of civil society. We already nominally belong to the current political system and need only to reposition (and perhaps redefine) ourselves in order to occupy mediating space. But the institutions that would allow our organizations to speak with a true public voice are, for the most part, still to be created. They have as their enemy not merely insufficient understanding but all the tantalizing seductions of the present system. How we cotton to the negative advertisements we affect to despise! How we feast on the incivilities of the tabloids we excoriate! This is our paradox: we need civility to help establish a civil society, but civility itself depends on behavior, attitudes, and institutions that only a civil society can create.

The revitalization of civil society is also intimately related to the status of work in our society. We have already noticed how easily civil society can be confused with the private market. The changing status of work in our time—and the gradual replacement of human labor by machines and electronics—challenges us and offers new opportunities for civil society. If sometime in the next century we are headed into an era "after work," the consequences for the arguments advanced here about democracy, civility, and civil society are likely to be absolutely decisive.

5

TIME, WORK, AND LEISURE
IN A CIVIL SOCIETY

Work, leisure, and civil society compete for a single scarce resource: time. How often we complain that we simply do not have enough hours in the day for the myriad civic and volunteer activities of the third sector when we are through with the demands of the other two. Some people seem to run to work to find the social pleasures no longer available in high-pressured two- and three-job families, while even the socially responsible insist politics (defined as voting, jury service, and tax-paying) already requires of them more public work than their schedules can afford. Here we stumble on a series of paradoxes that seem at once to encumber and to amplify the promise of civil society.

The first is the economic reality of jobs vanishing at the very moment when we are reaffirming the ideology of work, calling the work ethic our core value in the politics of welfare reform. Unemployment may be down, but employability is replacing employment, serial job-holding has taken the place of a career, and outsourced and consultancy style work has been substituted for full-time in-house work. The net result of these stealth forms of downsizing and disemployment is a labor force that enjoys a "full employment" economy only because it struggles to stay afloat in an insecure new workplace defined by ever-changing part-time, unpensioned, sometime jobs, often two or three per worker or per family. Many universities, for example, have taken advantage of retiring tenured professors who, counting the generous health and retirement benefits package, were earning up to $150,000 a year to teach four courses, by replacing them with itinerant graduate students or Ph.Ds who earn $10,000 ($2,500 per course) per year. Such beneficiaries of the soaring economy must take two or three such positions just to make ends meet, and they face the prospect of a lifetime of such piecework and will have to teach in several different institutions, carrying course loads three or four times as onerous as those of their well-paid tenured "colleagues," but without health or retirement benefits. They will pursue academic "careers" with no tenure, no permanent home, no collegiality, no loyalty from or to their institutions, and no relationship to their students (who will also be getting short-changed). But they will be "employed," and their fragmented professional lives may even yield two or more "jobs" in the Labor Department's glowing annual statistical reports on the full-employment economy.

Employers will of course claim they are merely seeking new flexible arrangements, "but what this means in reality," says Sara Horowitz, the director of the advocacy group Working Today, "is people are working increasingly without benefits. They're working not only without health coverage but without the protections of the major labor legislation of this century: pensions, minimum wage, occupational safety, unemployment insurance, age discrimination. The list goes on."[1] Nearly half of the part-time work force say they want to work more, and involuntary part-timers make significantly less than those who work part-time out of choice.[2]

Among those who are employed, the gap between rich and poor grows. This huge divide between the extremely well paid minority and a hard-working but ever less secure majority defines the new economic reality. Hence, on the one hand, sociologists like William Julius Wilson demonstrate that poverty and urban breakdown are the consequence of the disappearance of inner-city jobs, and, on the other, economists like Jeremy Rifkin prophesy a far graver disappearance of work as we know it, and a painful transition to a "near-workerless information society."[3] Industrial and service firms continue to downsize, and the traditional responses to increased productivity—opening up new economic sectors, for example, as when farm disemployment was compensated by new industrial jobs, or continuing economic growth—have reached their limit. The new information technology, highly specialized and automated, needs nothing like the vast army of workers once employed in agriculture, industry, and the service sector. In this new "regime of production," where computers have "increased exponentially the 'multiplied productive powers' of labor," the "principal effect of technological change—labor displacement—is largely unmitigated by economic growth."[4]

Yet, at this very point, anti-government and anti-welfare ideologists are demanding that work be the focal point in our solution to problems of poverty and welfare; and even the most progressive reformers are responding to corporate downsizing and the export of jobs with a vigorous (often protectionist) call for the "creation of good jobs for Americans in the United States"[5]—this, despite the fact that, as the journalist Thomas Friedman has said, "the bulk of job loss today is produced by technological change and deregulation and only 29 percent can be attributed to freer trade."[6] Scarce jobs are even under pressure from America's growing prison population (1.1 million today, more than triple what it was in 1980); the costs of incarceration ($25 billion a year) are offset by putting inmates to work,[7] and it is as if criminals are being authorized to continue their careers in prison, "stealing" jobs from the civilian population. New workfare programs also skim jobs from the shallow pool at the bottom of the economic ladder.

The second paradox is that while many people are disemployed in our society, those who work seem to be working harder than ever, giving labor an even greater value, and making "unearned" leisure seem more odious than ever before. One-third of the working force work more than forty-five hours a week, up from one-quarter just a few years ago.[8] Those who do not work at all understandably respond to their enforced free time with anger, passivity, despondency, or despair, making them poor candidates (despite their "leisure time") for volunteer activities. The culture of work compels them to seek relief in employment rather than creative leisure. "Before I was working, I was depressed all the time. I couldn't sleep at night," says a typical welfare-to-work success. As society applauds her display of industry in her new job, she exults, "Nowadays, I sleep like a baby."[9] If the unemployed are sleepless in their idleness, those still employed are frantic in their industriousness, leaving themselves little time for family or relaxation, let alone the demanding activities of civil society. No wonder that while participation in annual sign-a-check style "membership" organizations is up, participation in organizations requiring time and effort is down.[10]

The third and final paradox turns on contradictions in the voluntary part of civil society itself. While volunteerism is still prevalent in the United States and growing impressively elsewhere, a deep prejudice argues against linking it to income or incentives of any kind. The ideology that rejects welfare without work also criticizes voluntarism for pay or for educational vouchers. (As we have seen, this was a leading criticism of President Clinton's Learn and Serve Program at the Corporation for National Service.) The ethical asymmetry here means that while you should not get something (pay) without giving something (working!), you also should not get anything for giving. At the very time when linking income to voluntary service, homemaking, or other types of public work could solve the problems of vanishing work in the traditional industrial and service sectors, ideology condemns the solution.

These paradoxes arise out of beliefs about the nature of work and of income, about labor and human dignity, that have persisted for more than a millennium. They set culture and mores against the very solutions that in fact lie at hand. They manifest a cultural lag in which our values are stalled in the nineteenth century as our economy enters the twenty-first. The rehabilitation of civil society is promised by economic changes but it is sorely challenged by this cultural lag.

It was not always thus. For most of our history, through a providential symmetry, work for pay simultaneously yielded the income needed for men and women to survive and the productivity needed for economies to flourish. In our civilization, work has thus endowed human life with meaning, dignity, and status. Since economic health has been a condition for, as well as a consequence of, the growth of democracy, work has also been seen as undergirding the virtues of a free society. This link is manifest in the classical connection between the Protestant lionization of industry, thrift, and work and the growth of capitalist democracy.

But what appears in our history as an ineluctable economic law is in fact little more than a coincidence. The symmetry between those two epic achievements — income for individual workers, productivity for society at large — may seem to express a powerful moral logic: if a person is to eat, then surely that person must labor. Yet the moral logic evolved to fit the economic necessity, and the economic necessity is largely circumstantial, the contingent result of inefficiency and the limited historical productivity of labor as simple animal effort. Consumption and production have been linked in the wage relationship, but the conditions of consuming and producing have not. People need wages to sustain the buying power upon which their consumption in a market society depends, but productivity does not necessarily need wage earners to sustain it. After all, the mythic Eden into which our species was imagined to have been born offered prosperity without labor and fecundity without pain. The promise of a future Eden in which productivity again is a gift of divine imagination has quickened the pulse of economic utopians ever since, all the way down to Marx and Engels and their heirs. Friedrich Engels imagined a lifting of the economic yoke in which

> anarchy in social production is replaced by systematic, definite organization. The struggle for individual existence disappears. Then for the first time man, in a certain sense, is finally marked off from the rest of the animal kingdom, and emerges from mere animal conditions of existence into really human ones. . . . It is the ascent of man from the kingdom of necessity to the kingdom of freedom.[11]

The utopians dream on, but the realists dream only of more work. The decoupling of consumption and production through increased labor productivity and the intervention of efficient machines, if it comes to pass as historical actuality, is likely to be disruptive rather than utopian, a prelude to global unemployment and the spread of poverty rather than to global freedom and the spread of a civic culture in which human beings loosen the bonds of nature and truly become its lords.[12] The journalist William Greider, like Stanley Aronowitz before him, gloomily awaits a convergence of "cheap people and expensive machines" which, he believes, will produce a persistent oversupply of goods and undersupply of consumption—a "bidding war for employment" that allows global corporations to descend to "the bottom of the global wage" supply where there is a "seemingly inexhaustible supply of new recruits."[13]

Greider's dilemma—too much efficiency, increasing "labor arbitrage," fewer and fewer jobs, less income for workers and thus less cash for consumption, and so an even greater oversupply—is not easily addressed. This seemingly natural symmetry of work and income, of labor and prosperity, has meant that political and moral systems have grown up around the normative centrality of labor. Work has anchored our value system and centered our civic culture from the earliest days of the modern era. Protestants associated work with virtue because they believed it was God's price for redemption in the face of human sinfulness; John Locke's liberalism made it the key to all value, which he understood to arise out of the mixing of our self-owned bodily labor with nature's bounty and which he therefore viewed as a projection of our essential selves into the inert materials of the common world. Marx took this Lockean "labor theory of value" and converted it into a rationale for revolution, arguing that if men had to labor to earn wages, they deserved full title to everything their labor had created, the "surplus value" or profit left over after all the costs of production were paid. In our democracy today, work serves as a vital key to status, dignity, income, republican virtue, and most of the other things our society values. As Judith Shklar observed in her last (and most original) book, *American Citizenship*, the classical notion of public virtue, which equated citizenship with politics (the sovereign and noblest form of human activity), was quickly superseded in America by a "vision of economic independence, of self-directed 'earning' as the ethical basis of citizenship." We are, she noted, "citizens only if we 'earn.' "[4]

To this day, then, our political and moral regime is predicated on the notion that to be a responsible human being is to work, to be engaged in the production of those goods necessary to our common flourishing—feeding our family and fueling prosperity. Hence the paradoxes of a threatened age after work, when what should appear as a promised liberation in fact looms as a calamity. Ideology is unable to catch up to economic progress, and both progressives and conservatives cling to work as the key to morality and citizenship. Even a progressive commoner like James Carville writes in his populist polemic *We're Right, They're Wrong!*, "work and training for work are core values. They are the values that built this country."[15] For William Julius Wilson, the source of the ghetto's poverty as well as its despair is neither racism nor the collapse of families but the disappearance of work. The remedy for economic nationalists, social progressives, and radical egalitarians is jobs, jobs, and more jobs: old jobs, new jobs, traditional jobs, reengineered jobs, full-time jobs, part-time jobs, essential jobs, make-work jobs.[16]

Nothing new here. Given the traditional value system, modern progressivism has always campaigned not just for political emancipation and electoral suffrage but for economic justice, for jobs, and for fair and equitable wages. In the same spirit, but with an inverted political spin, modern conservatism has campaigned to assure that women and men do a day's work in return for whatever benefits they receive from the government. If we are to be paid fairly for work, we must work fairly for our pay, especially if "pay" takes the form of welfare or other government benefits. Welfare's moral entailment is workfare.

The recent rebellion against government-sponsored welfare programs has been a rebellion against the notion that people, even (or especially!) if they are teens with illegitimate babies, should somehow receive the wherewithal to live without "earning" it through work. "Earning" means doing paid labor, not homemaking or child-rearing or civic volunteering, not creating culture or enjoying freedom or filling leisure. Wages for labor in private-sector work has been the buckle linking work to income, labor to dignity, and employment to power and status. To work without adequate income is servitude of one kind, wage slavery, but to receive income without working is servitude of another: welfare dependency. These are the formulas by which the moral logic of work is played out in our democracy. This logic has turned our political parties into virtual twins, each devoted to one part of the formula linking income to "earning" and earning to work. Even when—other things being equal—we prefer that women stay at home with children ("family values"), we still believe that if the state pays the freight, mothers must carry the load and do something besides child care to "earn" their benefits. Work at private-sector jobs is obligatory. These moral calculations facilitated the economies of industrial-age societies in which labor power was still the key to productivity and growth, but they are disastrous for an information-age society where automation, robotics, and reengineering will offer productivity without labor and prosperity without jobs.

For all its seeming natural symmetry, the relationship between work and productivity has always been more contingent and variable than industrial-age ethics allowed. Not only have some labored while others did not (the reality of labor differentiation, the problem of distributive justice), but what counted as labor and what labor counted for have been contested. To the Greeks, labor by itself defined only mere animal existence, while leisure was the condition for freedom, politics, and truly "human" forms of being. Labor was relegated to animals, slaves, and (in the household) women, while citizens (men) enjoyed their freedom from private work by pursuing the public work of politics and culture, leaving private household economies to the drones. The gods, with whom they aspired to kinship, were divine creatures of leisure, not laborers in some Olympian vineyard. In his book *Leisure: The Basis of Culture*, Josef Pieper thus recalls that it was the gods "taking pity on mankind, born to work," who decreed festivals and leisure time so that in the company of the muses "they might nourish themselves in festive companionship" and so "again stand upright and erect."[17] Hannah Arendt and other German and American celebrants of classical republicanism have always distinguished man the laborer (*homo laborans*) from his nobler cousins man the actor, maker, and playful creator (*homo faber, homo ludens*), whose creative and productive activity established him as more than a mere instrument of bodily labor.[18] In Aristotle's view, man the contemplative philosopher manifested the highest form of virtue, seeking the ennobling leisure of contemplative gods.

With the passing of classical republicanism, bodily work was integrated into civic value systems, while leisure became associated with what in classical times was its very opposite—slothfulness. Enough of the classical world's utopian humanism remained, however, to keep alive the quest for liberation from the yoke of labor. The history of production has thus been a history of labor's growing productivity, augmented by machines, first mechanical and then electronic and digital. Increased efficiency inevitably meant decreased dependency on human labor. The ox did the work of many men, the wheel multiplied the efficiency of the ox, the steam and internal-combustion engines enhanced the efficacy of the wheel. Each increment in efficiency decreased the claims of industry on human labor and represented another step on the journey to liberation. Where classical democracy had allowed the few to enjoy leisure on the backs of slavery, had allowed the liberty of the few to depend on the servitude of the many, and freedom to be a product of inequality, now there appeared the promise of liberty for all, rooted in the emancipation of productivity from human labor altogether—Engels's "ascent to the kingdom of freedom," Nietzsche's heroic realm of self-invented men.

Hence today, when we can foresee an "end of work" and none of us can deny that the requirements of human labor have been radically transformed by automation, what once seemed a natural fact of human existence looks more and more like a coincidental outcome of inefficiency that can be and is being overcome. When just a little more than a century ago most Americans labored on farms to produce enough food for their own fellow citizens alone, today less than 2 percent of us feed all of America and much of the world besides. No one thinks she is morally compelled to cultivate her own garden in order to be entitled to eat, or to grow with her own hands the food she feeds her own children.

The industrial economy lags behind agriculture by a century or two, but the advent of automation permits a reengineeering of industrial society where an ever diminishing proportion of us will be able to produce the goods and services needed by the growing world population.[19] For even service jobs are subject to automation, as anyone who once depended on secretaries, bank tellers and telephone operators knows. Surely the question is no longer *if* but only *when* the trends of our economy mandating what Jeremy Rifkin has called the end of work as we know it will dominate our economic and civic institutions.

Yet we still think, in the old way, that entitlement rests on labor contribution. Through the device of wage labor, the incomes of women and men as consumers are directly related to their participation in production, whether or not production requires their presence. And the economic participation defined by work is not just crucial to income and consumption but suffuses democracy's most visible values: status, power, and dignity. As once in the nineteenth century the populist progressive Eugene Debs could aver that "the man who by honest toil earns an honest living is a peer of the realm," so the modern populist progressive James Carville affirms: "I believe with all my heart that outside of love and faith, the most sacred thing you can render in this world is your labor."[20] Accordingly, the neo-liberal Micky Kaus calls for a new "civic liberalism" in which

> liberals would, in effect, make work the prerequisite for full citizenship. The work ethic could assume its place as the basis of a unifying, egalitarian culture in which the affluent as well as the poor judge themselves, not by how much money they make but by whether they are pulling their weight.[21]

But the trouble with Kaus's formula is that the weight of the modern economy is already being pulled by machines and computers and robots and does not require that women and men stay in harness to draw "their" weight—which is "theirs" no longer for some pertinent economic reason but only for moral and psychological reasons that continue to sacralize work.

When work for pay has this sacred aspect, then decoupling work from productivity, which the modern economy has done, becomes a sacrilege, a rabid secular heresy, and it challenges our political, economic, and social institutions. How should we deal with a flourishing economy in which an increasing percentage of the work force is cast as mere spectators? What once happened to a farm economy, which went in a century from employing nearly 80 percent of the population to employing but 2 percent, is happening in the industrial economy today, and it will happen in the service sector in the years to come. As Jeremy Rifkin puts it: "The wholesale substitution of machines for workers is going to force the very nation to rethink the role of human beings in the social process. Redefining opportunities and responsibilities for millions of people in a society absent of mass formal employment is likely to be the single most pressing social issue of the coming century."[22] Yet the new enforced leisure seems heretical in the face of work's traditional sanctity, while "technical" solutions of the kind proffered by Rifkin and other economists are unlikely to succeed if they smack of sloth, or if they "privilege" those who do not "earn a living" yet are supported in their living anyway.

We have to find new ways to distribute the fruits of nonlabor-based productivity to the general population, *whether or not they work for their living*. Otherwise, more and more citizens will become poor in economic and social terms (low income, low status), and the system itself, capable theoretically of surviving without an extensive work force, will be undermined and destroyed by political instability, new forms of class war, and—most ironic of all—by not enough income-earning consumers to buy all the goods in this labor-free world. The system will fail not because of economic inadequacy but because of hyper-adequacy: its capacity to function efficiently and productively without significant labor input. Once it has failed, the only means to break this kind of logjam will be Malthusian: catastrophes of starvation, inequality, civil strife, and war that reduce the population and break the economic machine in ways that eventually create new jobs. But ending civilization as we have known it over five thousand years does not seem a very efficient way to deal with downsizing. Do we have an alternative?

Imagine a world in which only one in two or perhaps one in five work to produce goods sufficient to the needs of the others. Unemployed and desalaried, how will the others benefit from the remarkable productivity of the few who still work? (These latter will of course for the most part be knowledge workers — what Robert Reich calls symbolic-analyst workers.) Current assumptions tend to give credit to executives and shareholders for increased efficiencies, leaving workers to suffer the consequences of downsizing. But what are all those workers who are no longer needed to do to gain status in society? to "earn" a living that society will be able to afford to give them for free? to share in the efficiencies they helped to create but which now render them superfluous? to occupy their leisure time without feeling lazy or despondent? to feel independent and worthy of the goods that an efficient system of economic distribution will eventually have to make available to all, whether or not they work?

The dependency syndrome that stalks the lives of welfare recipients in our time demonstrates how bleak and demeaning it is to live without work in a world whose chief values are still defined by it. Indeed, the rush of middle-class women into paid work over the last several decades, as part of their search for status and dignity, suggests just how impoverished nonwork occupations outside the private-market sector have become. And this has occurred just when private-market labor is becoming economically redundant, just when public forms of work — community service, child rearing, cultural or civic efforts, the work of play—are needed more than ever.

"From each according to ability, to each according to need" had a radical ring in the nineteenth century. But what if nothing at all is required "from" most of us, while all of us go on having more and more "needs" that can be filled without our contributing anything? How much more radical it is to proclaim: "From each, nothing at all, in return for the fulfillment of all your needs!" And how much more morally disruptive! Gain without pain? Bounty absent the sweat of bent brows? Eden regained? Yet the decoupling of work and productivity suggests the need for just such peculiar and ironic moral formulas.

To be sure, interim remedies can be found in technical economic adjustments that continue to value work. And were global population control ever to produce a significant population decline, it is conceivable that the global labor oversupply might be reduced (although at the price of fewer potential consumers, too). Interim adjustments are already being experimented with in Europe. As the growing productivity decreases the number of jobs, the remaining ones can be carved up and reparceled more equitably.

Lionel Jospin's socialist government in France has introduced a law mandating a thirty-five-hour work week for all French workers by the year 2000, with no diminution of wages, on the controversial theory that it will produce more jobs; as insurance, he is also proposing to create 700,000 new positions, half of them in the civil society sector (the government bearing 80 percent of the cost and the private sector 20 percent), an innovation that would give official status to the idea of "public work" as wage-worthy labor. Under the pressure of a strike, the government has also legislated early-retirement opportunities for truckers. Early retirement takes workers out of the marketplace, making room for the young, but it also taxes an already overburdened social security system. Indeed, the problem the Prime Minister will eventually face is how to pay for these conscientious innovations, especially if downsizing offsets whatever gains in jobs the thirty-five-hour week and a shorter working career may bring. Still, Jospin's economic plan is the first in the Western world to recognize that employment, public sector work, and leisure are responsibilities of government no less pressing than those of the productivity and profitability of business.

Elsewhere in Europe, both the state and the private sectors are pursuing technical solutions to the labor market crisis. Automobile companies in Germany (Volkswagen and BMW, for example) have agreed to shorten work schedules and reduce the work week to under thirty hours in return for union concessions.[23] At least some of the growing anti-foreigner sentiment in Austria, Germany, and Switzerland arises out of a fear of disemployment—even though many guest workers do unskilled labor natives have traditionally refused to do. More than twenty years ago, I urged that jobs be divided where feasible, so that women and men could continue to work half time for a single family wage, allowing them both to be involved in their families as well as their workplaces—an idea also championed by Betty Friedan and others.[24]

The Clinton Administration under the leadership of former Labor Secretary Robert Reich committed itself to job retraining and education for multiple careers. The wishful and wistful assumption here was that the problem was the export of jobs, not their diminishing number globally. It is certainly true that unemployment in the United States today is remarkably low, and some will argue that the "decline of work" is an illusion, a short-term effect of another shift in market and economic production of the kind that drove millions of agricultural workers from the fields in the late nineteenth century, only to see them resurface and achieve new success in industrial cities a few decades later. There are not, however, an infinite number of new economic sectors. And the "people" jobs in the service sector, where much of the employment slack is being taken up, are subject to automation. In any case, many of these new jobs are part-time and underpaid, without the traditional benefits of a full-time industrial job, and they have less significance in an economy where families share two or three jobs to scratch out a living that a single job might once have provided.

The smart talk about "life-time employability" rather than life-time employment is a way of disguising the increasing marginality of labor in the information economy. Talk about the booming economy and endless jobs rings hollow to workers, more than two-thirds of whom reported in a recent survey that "despite the best economic conditions in a generation . . . their sense of job security is lower and their job stress higher than it used to be."[25] With corporations' share of national income up to a near record of 11 percent, and (with real wages falling) labor's share of corporate profits down to 8 percent, their perceptions are accurate.[26] Even Federal Reserve Chairman Alan Greenspan, as enthusiastic a booster of the current economy as we are likely to find, has said, "It is one thing to believe that the economy, indeed the job market, will do well overall, but quite another to feel secure about one's individual situation, given the accelerated pace of corporate re-structuring and the heightened fear of skill obsolescence that has apparently characterized this expansion."[27]

Joblessness is a problem for producers as well as laborers, for the former understand that the latter are also consumers. At the very beginning of the age of mass production, Henry Ford observed that unless those who made his cars earned enough to buy them, their productivity would be wasted and the automobile industry would fail. Nothing has changed: even if a day comes when cars can be made without significant human labor power at all, they cannot be sold unless consumers can afford to buy them—whether with wages or with some other form of income by which the benefits of efficient productivity are distributed. Yet when producers need far fewer employees than consumers, their tactical maneuvering can only be halfhearted. They continue to downsize even as they wring their hands. They persist in talking about "growth" and new jobs even as they merge. Will Boeing and McDonnell-Douglas really keep all the jobs that two independent companies provided, now that they are a single company searching for efficiencies to make their merger profitable?[28] The United Parcel Service settled on a new contract with the Teamsters with terms favorable to the latter, but UPS had to downsize to pay for its concessions. The result? Better-paid but fewer jobs, and another installment in the story of economic polarization.

Indeed, nearly all the prudent tactical adjustments one can imagine share a common defect: they ignore the long-term implications for work of the automated knowledge-based economy, and consequently they compete for and try (in what can only be futile ways) to distribute and divide and retrain for an ever-diminishing number of jobs. Shorter work weeks, Roosevelt-era WPA-style government-sponsored jobs, restrictions on self-service such as New Jersey's ban on pumping your own gas, split and shared jobs, early retirement, and education and retraining programs may delay the onset of the value crisis, but they cannot restore work to its previous place of honor, or provide anything like the number of long-term, full-wage, pension- and insurance-carrying jobs that industrial capitalism generated at its labor-intensive pinnacle. In the long run, work itself must either be redefined or severed completely from income, so that human welfare does not depend on labor to get (not "earn") a "living."

The pernicious effect of the end of work on status and dignity can be only temporarily deferred by economic remedies. A permanent improvement requires society to decouple income from production, consumers from producers, work from entitlement. This would be a momentous and monumental transformation of our work-linked civic value system. And however feasible it may become in technical economic terms (Rifkin, Aronowitz, and oth-

ers describe several prudent strategies for the transition), there are
daunting political and moral hurdles. And it would require a revision of the moral logic which for centuries has made work the
source of virtue and civic entitlement.

Can a civilization built around wage labor undergo such a con-
version? Can our workaholic society dissociate leisure from pejor-
ative linkages to the "leisure classes," to laziness, and to economic
parasitism? Champions of leisure from Aristotle to Sebastian de
Grazia who have seen in it the foundations of intellectual virtue
and the very source of our civilization have tried to pry it apart
from the association with sloth and inactivity.[29] But cultures like
ours suffused with the work ethic find it difficult to appreciate the
difference. They seem likely to continue to view women and men
without jobs as economic parasites feeding off the labor of others,
even when there are no jobs for them to fill and no good economic
reason for them to earn through work the income the hyper-
productive economy needs them to receive in order for them to
be efficient consumers (and what they need to live).

The challenge is political as well as economic. We need moral
grounds and civic reasons to reinforce the new economic logic in
which work and productivity are severed. Here is where the dilemmas of civil society in the age of McWorld's global economy — too
little time and space for third-sector activity — can give us hope.
For if the linkage of work and wages has accounted for many of
our civilization's virtues, it has also been the source of a paramount
vice: in monopolizing time and defining status in terms of labor
alone, work has crowded out our social and civic agenda. Democracy depends on leisure, on time to be educated into civil society,
time to participate in deliberation, time to serve on juries, occupy
municipal magistracies, volunteer for civic activities. Wilde was
right: there weren't enough free evenings to accommodate his radical political principles; and advocates of civil society must worry
about securing afternoons and weekends as well. Unable both to

work and to participate in democracy, we were led to depend on representative institutions where others did the work of governance for us. The "iron law" dictating that representative government would inevitably become oligarchical is rooted largely in the inability of those represented to find time to oversee and get involved in self-governance. The early democratic republics of our civilization, understanding democracy to mean self-government in a strictly literal sense, demanded much of their citizens, and flourished only inasmuch as citizens were released from the burdens of labor. In Athens, our first "free society," it was ironically a system of slavery that permitted free Athenians to be full-time citizens. They were free to debate the peace and fight the wars because slaves did the work and produced the goods. In early Switzerland, where a communal version of direct democracy was established over seven hundred years ago, it was a pastoral economy that left long winters of leisure in which the free Swiss could cultivate their institutions and establish peasant armies capable of defending their mountain fortress as well as serving the mercenary needs of neighbors.

By contrast, the peasant agricultural societies of the rest of Europe, steeped in endless work, were producing what Edward Banfield later called a morally backward society weighed down by drudgery and defined by passivity. Karl Marx identified such features of the agricultural society with what he called the "idiocy of rural life": indenture to the soil as prelude to more human forms of bondage like wage slavery. Sunrise-to-sundown labor leaves little time in which to practice civic statecraft or indulge the apprenticeship of liberty, and it abandons the muses of art to commerce and to an inevitable commercialization of culture. Industrial societies have done little better in managing time: the proletariat has for the most part found precious little room in its endless days of hard labor and long decades of drudgery either for revolution or for reform, let alone for civility or for culture, content today to be

placated with electronic circuses. Working, shopping, watching—
the job place, the mall, and the television—leave neither time nor
place for politics or art or civic culture, except in the lives of the
disemployed and disempowered. But the disillusion and despondency of spreading unemployment have been felt more as spurs to
despair than opportunities for civic engagement or edifying leisure. The women and men who have the most to gain from suffrage are those least likely to practice it, even if only once a year.[30]
Nor, short of a cultural and moral transformation, are the unemployed and the welfare poor likely to respond to marginalization
by spending their free time in civic voluntarism or cultural self-
improvement.

How very cunning the cunning of reason is: at the very moment
the human race finally stands on the threshold of the workless
world for which it has labored these many millennia, it turns and
flees in horror back into servitude. Give us back our chains! it
cries. Take back the liberty the miraculous achievements of technology proffer and give us, instead, jobs! We would rather work
than face the greater burden of freedom, than reembrace a democratic civil society or give up private labor in the name of economic survival and shoulder the weight of public work in the name
of human improvement.

Democracy's logic is clear: if productivity has demanded work
and work has become associated with status and power, democracy
has demanded leisure but, in its modern absence, has had to settle
for second-class representative institutions. In societies where the
title "wage earner" brings more respect than the title "citizen," who
can blame people for adopting a moral code in which voting is
discretionary but work mandatory? By tying civic virtue to the labor
of shopkeepers and yeoman farmers, by tying citizenship to
property-holding and the A-type Calvinist habits that made it possible, America's early republicans knit together a leisureless work
economy with the thinner civic virtues of a representative democ-

racy. Their strategy has today become part of the problem. Judith
Shklar has incisively demonstrated that work is more crucial to the
core values of our democracy than anything else. But, under those
conditions, labor's diminishing role in the face of the post-modern
economy's efficiency becomes not merely an economic but a political issue. The end of work threatens the end of civic status and
the end of dignity as well.

Here is where our two stories intersect to produce a quite miraculous prospect. The story of rising, ever more efficient productivity which renders human labor redundant converges with the
tale of vanishing civic time in the face of government and market
gargantuanism: here there is a unique opportunity for the restitu-
tion of civic life. Where the stories converge, the downsizing and
unemployment associated with labor obsolescence in a post-
modern hyper-efficient economy are transformed into the promise
of a civil society, a leisure society in which civic culture is finally
cut loose from commerce and made the focus of citizens liberated
from work. The commercial malls that have encroached on our
civic space can be rolled back by political will, as the commercialization of time that has filled our days with labor is rolled back
by economic necessity.

The final victory of emancipation through work is emancipation
from work. Forced for eons to earn its daily bread by the sweat of
bent brows in a place East of Eden, humankind is abruptly offered
an escape back into the garden in which human needs are largely
met through the products not of human labor but of human imagination. For machines and robotics and computers are human
imagination made manifest, a surrogate for Eden's bountiful God
that frees us to enjoy imagination as an end in itself—education,
play, politics, and art as forms of association and creativity. Private
market work gives way to public and civic work, activity on behalf
of art and family, neighborhood and polity, religion and school.[31]
We are given the opportunity to use labor's material gifts to pursue

not just material needs (shopping!) but civilization—if we can remember that work is the instrument and culture the object and
can wean ourselves from the seductive tyrannies of production and
consumption.

The strategies we require here are not economic and technical
but political and cultural: making hobbies as rewarding as work,
making civic volunteering as income-producing as commercial labor, making just distribution a function of need, making imagination a faculty worthy of remuneration, making art and culture
objects of social support, making high-quality education—above
all, civic education—accessible to all. The economic strategies fol-
low: once the political will is in place to decouple work and reward, many feasible innovations are possible—for example, the law
professor Bruce Ackerman's proposal for a once-in-a-lifetime capital
grant to all people to create a stake-holders' society in which everyone is economically vested, or Tony Atkinson's idea of a "participation income" that would be pegged to civic engagement of every
kind, and would separate the distribution of productivity's earnings
from wage labor (a proposal in which Tony Blair's new Labour
government in Britain has shown some interest).[32] But first a
change in deep cultural perspective is needed.

At this moment, standing on the threshold of a new era, those
with time on their hands should feel no shame in their hearts.
Their unwanted leisure can be the occasion for more than envy,
or depression, or lassitude, or simple rage, which they feel only
because we have equated the active life exclusively with labor activity in the market sector. Even at play, we "labor" with an industry that robs us of leisure's succor and its promise. But public
and civic work, as well as homemaking and family work, should
not be discretionary, while wage-earning market labor is obligatory.
Quite the other way around.

At present, the disemployed and underemployed and unemployed—whether mothers or homemaking fathers, downsized in-

formation society cast-offs or hard-core welfare cases — hardly can be considered a leisure class in potentia, ready to enter the "kingdom of freedom." "Our future," writes the economist Lester C. Thurow, "is the masterless American laborer, wandering from employer to employer, unable to build a career."[33] But Thurow's pessimism depends on a work-centered culture in which status and dignity usually disappear along with work, and the only "career" worth talking about is a wage-earning workplace career, in which leisure time is thought of as an evasion of rather than an opportunity to assume responsibility and civic obligations. Feminism has had a difficult time with homemaking because the home lacks both the pecuniary rewards and the public virtues of the economic workplace. Even cultural conservatives who celebrate family values are outraged by women without providers who stay home to raise children: thus the universal drive to compel welfare mothers to "work," even where there are neither appropriate jobs available nor an economic need for their labor, and even where their "work" at home might yield greater benefits for their children and for society at large.

To be fired, to be a housewife, to be a welfare mother, or to be a homemaker, to be unemployed or to be an unpaid civic volunteer, is in every case to be without power, without status, and without entitlement; and thus without dignity. The transformation of the role of work in our economic system will hence have to await the transvaluation of our civic and moral systems — something at which we will have to "work" exactly in this new public sense.[34] Those with time on their hands are potentially our most promising citizens. Homemakers and retired folks and those no longer "needed" by an efficient production system are more needed than ever by civil society. Freed from the onus of contributing to economic capital, women and men can become potential creators of social capital. In the age after work, democracy can rediscover the missing citizens stolen from it by the long epoch of value squeezed from labor. Civil society can finally have its own work force. Democracy can be our most magnanimous employer. Citizenship can again be the most human of all occupations.

If history has then conspired against civility in the manner portrayed here—squeezing civil society between the hammer of big government and the anvil of markets—it appears now to be conspiring with it. In a provocative realization of Marx's prophecy anticipating a new world of abundance no longer rooted in endless labor, our society is moving toward conditions that could nourish the resuscitation of civil society—not just public work but public play, cultural leisure as well as civic labor, fun no less than ferment, the joys of living in place of the burdens of earning a living. And the question we face, it becomes ever more apparent, is not whether history will permit the rehabilitation of civil society, but whether we habit-mired human beings will be able to make good on history's promise and, through acts of bold political imagination and moral transformation, convert the deficits of a world after work into the assets of a flourishing democracy—a civil society that is once again truly a place for us.

NOTES

INTRODUCTION

1. Walt Whitman, "By Blue Ontario's Shore," *Leaves of Grass*.

2. Michael Walzer, "The Idea of Civil Society," *The Kettering Review*, Winter 1997, p. 8. Originally the Gunnar Myrdal Lecture, delivered in Sweden in 1990 and published in *Dissent* in 1991.

3. Alexis de Tocqueville, *Democracy in America*.

4. Among those working papers was a small piece of this book in an earlier version.

5. See *The New Democrat*, 7(2) (March/April 1995), special issue on Civil Society, and also George Liebmann's *The Little Platoons: Local Governments in Modern History* (1995) for an account from the center left; Senator Dan Coats, "Can Congress Revive Civil Society?" *Policy Review*, Jan./Feb. 1996, for a view from the right. Also see the new second edition of the classic work by Peter Berger and John Neuhaus, *To Empower People: The Role of Mediating Structures in Public Policy* (1977).

6. In this spirit, Bronislaw Geremek writes: "The concept of civil society appeared fairly late in the annals of Central and Eastern European resistance to communism . . . as a program of resistance in Poland during the late 1970's and 1980's." "Civil Society and the Present Age," in *The Idea of Civil Society* (1992), p. 11.

7. See Robert Putnam, "Bowling Alone: America's Declining Social Capital,"

Journal of Democracy, 6(1):65 (Jan. 1995); Francis Fukuyama, *Trust: Social Virtues and the Creation of Prosperity* (1995); Amitai Etzioni, ed., *New Communitarian Thinking* (1995); Michael Sandel, *Democracy's Discontent: In Search of a Public Philosophy* (1996); and Joseph S. Nye, Jr., Philip Zelikow, and David King, eds., *Why People Don't Trust Government* (1997). Related arguments are found in Senator Dan Coats, *Policy Review*, Jan./Feb. 1996; Harry Boyte and Benjamin Barber, *Civic Declaration—A Call for a New Citizenship: A New Citizenship Project of the American Civic Forum*, Dec. 9, 1994, an Occasional Paper of The Kettering Foundation; Harry Boyte and Nancy Kiri, *Building America: The Democratic Promise of Public Work* (1996). The charge of "decline" in trust and membership is a controversial one, especially in the form it has been put by Putnam. For the debate, see *The American Prospect*, Winter 1996.

8. The national PTA is down from nearly 12 million members in 1960 to just over 7 million in 1990. Putnam's data make the case over a broad spectrum of membership groups, arguing that only in passive membership organizations like the AARP and the Sierra Club, where check-writing is the primary "activity," is the trend different.

1. THREE KINDS OF CIVIL SOCIETY

1. There is no fully adequate account of civil society's philosophical genealogy. Andrew Arato and Jean Cohen offer a penetrating and broad-ranging account in their *Civil Society and Political Theory* (1992), but at a level of philosophical sophistication and with a focus on the European experience that may be daunting to the general reader. An excellent collection of essays that also discloses the contours of the European debate is Adolf Bibic and Gigi Graziano, *Civil Society, Political Society, Democracy* (1994). Adam B. Seligman's account of the history of the idea (in his *The Idea of Civil Society*, 1992) is more accessible but is marred by episodes of uncertain scholarship and peculiar biases against current political debates about civil society that perhaps arise from Seligman's preoccupation with eastern Europe and his seeming ignorance of the practical political character of the debate in the United States. (Also, the most interesting current debates got under way after his book was completed.) Seligman also makes a foolish attempt to distinguish the prescriptive and descriptive in ways that obscure his arguments.

2. See, for example, Arato and Cohen, *Civil Society and Political Theory*.

3. Stansislaw Baranczak, "On the Role of Artists and Intellectuals," in *The Idea of Civil Society* (1992), p. 10.

4. Robert Nozick, *Anarchy, State and Utopia* (1974), p. ix. This variety of lib-

ertarianism has an anarchist tinge to it and, with its Nietzschean overtones, recalls radical works like Max Stirner's nineteenth-century tract *The Ego and Its Own* (recently edited by David Leopold, 1995).

5. See, for example, Karl Popper, *The Open Society and Its Enemies* (1952); and Judith N. Shklar, "The Liberalism of Fear," in Nancy Rosenblum, ed., *Liberalism and the Moral Life* (1989).

6. Both "On Markets and Privatization," in *The Idea of Civil Society*, p. 8.

7. Richard Rorty, *Contingency, Irony, and Solidarity* (1989), p. 61.

8. *Centesimus Annus* (1991). The Pope recognizes three, not two domains, and emphasizes the function of civil society in rescuing the individual from being crushed between the "two poles of the state and the market."

9. See Amitai Etzioni, ed., *New Communitarian Thinking: Persons, Virtues, Institutions, and Communities* (1995), and Michael Lerner, *The Politics of Meaning: Restoring Hope and Possibility in an Age of Cynicism* (1996).

10. Haider regularly refers to elected officials and their appointees as "functionaries of coercive institutions" and "inflexible bureaucratic monsters" whose politics stand in the way of real people's democracy. Jörg Haider, *Befreite Zukunft jenseits von links und rechts: Menschliche Alternativen für eine Brücke ins neue Jahrtausend* (1997), p. 23. Haider's very title—"A Liberated Future, Beyond Left and Right: Human Alternatives on the Bridge [sic!] to the new millennium"—apes the transpartisanship of new communitarian usage and pays solicitous homage to leaders like President Clinton. Thus does the new communitarian right in Europe try to bury its prejudices in the soothing rhetoric of civil-society nonpartisanship.

11. See *The Uses of Disorder: Personal Identity and City Life* (1970) and *The Fall of Public Man* (1977).

12. See Robert Nisbet, *The Twilight of Authority* (1975), Peter Berger and John Neuhaus (note 5 in the introduction), and Alan Ehrenhalt, *The Lost City* (1995).

13. The death-trap image is from Michael Lesy's *Wisconsin Death Trip* (1973). On the dark side, Thomas Hardy offers a disconcerting feel for the intolerance that can define a village community in *Jude the Obscure*, while Toni Morrison's *Bluest Eye* is unsentimentally savage about the kind of impoverished African-American family that might have once been the subject of nostalgia. See also Sherwood Anderson's *Winesburg, Ohio*.

14. Michael Oakeshott, *On Human Conduct* (1975), p. 239.

15. Peter Laslett's *The World We Have Lost* (1965) gives a philosopher's idealized and nostalgic account of life in face-to-face village communities in Britain in the sixteenth and seventeenth centuries.

16. Adam Smith, *An Inquiry into the Nature and Causes of the Wealth of Nations,* Edwin Cannan, ed. (1976), II, 314. By multiplying sects, Smith writes, one can nurture in society both "good temper and moderation."

2. A PLACE FOR US

1. Michael Sandel, *Democracy's Discontent* (1996), p. 5.

2. Although they do not much discuss "the relationship between work and citizenship and democracy," Boyte and Kari observe that "people become creators of their communities, stakeholders in the country, and guardians of the commonwealth through common work." Harry C. Boyte and Nancy N. Kari, *Building America: The Democratic Promise of Public Life* (1996), pp. 2–3. Boyte might rebel at being regarded as a civic republican, but his concerns with commonwealth (see his *Commonwealth: A Return to Citizen Politics,* 1989), public work, and citizenship represent an important interpretation of civil society that is neither liberal nor communitarian.

3. Sandel, p. 6.

4. See Sara Evans and Harry Boyte, *Free Spaces: The Sources of Democratic Change in America* (1992).

5. For a debate on the place of service between government and markets, see Williamson Evers, ed., *National Service: Pros and Cons* (1990).

6. Boyte and Kari, *Building America*, p. 5.

7. Civicus, *The New Civic Atlas: Profiles of Civil Society in Sixty Countries* (1997), p. vii.

8. See *Hungary: A Civil Approach: A Survey of the Hungarian Nonprofit Sector* (1997), p. 9. In 1932, Hungary had nearly 15,000 civil associations that disappeared during the years of fascism, war, and communism.

9. See James Fishkin, *Democracy and Deliberation* (1992). Theodore L. Becker and his colleagues have developed effective pilots in which electronic voting is tempered by various deliberative strategies. See Becker's pioneering work on the Hawaiian and Californian televotes, available from the University of North Carolina; also his "Televote: Interactive, Participatory Polling," in Becker and R. A. Couto, *Teaching Democracy by Being Democratic* (1996).

10. Michael Walzer, "The Idea of Civil Society, *The Kettering Review,* Winter 1997, p. 21.

11. Nicholas Eberstadt, "World Population Implosion," *The Public Interest,* cited by Ben J. Wattenberg, "The Population Explosion is Over," *The New York Times Magazine,* Nov. 23, 1997, p. 63.

12. See M. A. Glendon and David Blankenhorn, *Seedbeds of Virtue* (1995).

13. In the header for an essay by Alan Cowell, "Like it or Not, Germany Becomes a Melting Pot," *The New York Times*, Nov. 30, 1997.

14. Rorty, *Contingency, Irony, and Solidarity*, p. 64.

15. Petr Pajas, "Czech Republic," in *The New Civic Atlas*, p. 32.

3. MAKING CIVIL SOCIETY REAL

1. See Senator Dan Coats, "Can Congress Revive Civil Society?" *Policy Review*, Jan./Feb. 1996.

2. See "Harnessing Technology for Development" (The World Bank, 1997).

3. Montaville Flowers, *America Chained* (1931).

4. Sandel, *Democracy's Discontent*, p. 229. It was not a stretch, Michael Sandel shows, to get from such concerns to anxiety about how catalogues from Sears, Roebuck and Montgomery Ward could destroy the independence of farmers. When Justice Hugo Black was still a senator, he condemned the "wild craze for efficiency in production, sale, and distribution [that] has swept over the land, increasing the number of the unemployed, building up a caste system, dangerous to any government. Chain groceries, chain dry-goods stores, chain clothing stores, here today and merged tomorrow, grow in size and power . . . The local man and merchant is passing and his community loses his contribution to local affairs as an independent thinker and executive" (Cited in Boorstin, *The Americans*, pp. 111–12).

5. "The Small Business as a School of Manhood," in *Atlantic Monthly*, Vol. 93, 1904.

6. Citation from Sandel, p. 74.

7. Brandeis, *Business: A Profession* (reprint, 1996), pp. 252–53.

8. Humphrey asked in 1952: "Do we want an America where the economic market place is filled with a few Frankensteins and giants? Or do we want an America where there are thousands upon thousands of small entrepreneurs, independent businessmen, and landholders who can stand on their own feet and talk back to their Government or to anyone else?" Senate Debate, 82nd Congress, 2nd session, July 1–2, 1952.

9. Sandel, pp. 94–95.

10. "The Global Citizen," *The Berkshire Eagle*, Aug. 14, 1995.

11. Steven Greenhouse, "Measure to Ban Import Items," *The New York Times*, Oct. 1, 1997.

12. The White House collaborated in this initiative in the spirit of its voluntary

Model Business Principles, issued by the Department of Commerce in 1996, and aimed at "provision of a safe and healthful workplace, fair employment practices, and responsible environmental protection" (Department of State Publication 10486, Washington, D.C., June 1997). This administrative jawboning is welcome but does not by itself constitute a sufficient consumer-side strategy. In his 1998 State of the Union Address, Clinton proposed a program to ban child labor globally.

13. See Peter Applebome, "Plan Adds Civil Education to the Basics of Schooling, *The New York Times*, Monday, April 24, B8.

14. For details, see Richard M. Battistoni, *Experiencing Citizenship*: *Concepts and Models for Service Learning in Political Science* (1997), and my *An Aristocracy of Everyone* (1994).

4. CIVILITY AND CIVILIZING DISCOURSE

1. This section borrows in part from my "An American Civic Forum," in *Social Philosophy and Policy*, Vol. 13, No. 1, Winter 1996, pp. 269–83.

2. "The tree of liberty must be refreshed from time to time with the blood of patriots and tyrants. It is the natural manure." Thomas Jefferson, Letter to Colonel Smith, Nov. 13, 1787.

3. See Boyte and Evans, *Free Spaces: The Sources of Democratic Change in America*, 19.

5. TIME, WORK, AND LEISURE

1. Cited by Steven Greenhouse, "Item in Tax Bill Poses Threat to Job Benefits," *The New York Times*, July 20, 1997, p. 18. The formula corporations have used to "restructure" the workplace has been to reclassify employees as "consultants" and "independent contractors"—which allows firms to stop paying pension, health, and other traditional benefits.

When asked whether they preferred higher pay or sustained benefits, 62 percent of workers polled in one survey reported they would rather keep their benefits than have a pay raise.

2. Robert Kuttner, "Take the High Road on Labor," *The Berkshire Eagle*, Aug. 10, 1997, p. A9. Kuttner reports that Manpower, Inc., the temp agency, is today America's largest employer. See also Chris Tilly, *Half a Job*.

3. William Julius Wilson, *When Work Disappears: The World of the New Urban Poor* (1996); and Jeremy Rifkin, *The End of Work* (1995), p. 59.

4. Stanley Aronowitz and William DiFazio, *The Jobless Future: Sci-Tech and*

the Dogma of Work (1994), p. 21. "In the wake of the shrinking social wage, joblessness, the supplanting of good full-time jobs by mediocre badly paid part-time jobs tends to thwart the ability of the economic system to avoid chronic overproduction and underconsumption." This is the theme explored in the setting of the global economy by William Greider in his *One World, Ready or Not* (1997).

5. Kenneth M. Dolbeare and Janette K. Hubble, *USA 2012: After the Middle Class Revolution* (1996), p. 89.

6. Thomas L. Friedman, "Down With Chips!" *The New York Times*, Oct. 6, 1997.

7. "Need Work? Go to Jail," *U.S. News and World Report*, Dec. 9, 1996, p. 66.

8. Figures from a Princeton Survey Research Associates Poll, *U.S.A. Today*, cover story, Aug. 29, 1997. The poll revealed that in 1997 33 percent of the work force worked more than forty-five hours a week, up from 27 percent six years earlier. In 1991, Juliet Schor found that Americans were working on average 163 more hours (nearly an extra month) per year in 1990 than they had in 1970 (Juliet Schor, *The Overworked American*, 1991). This increase in working hours is not due to a growing zest for work, but the result of families "trapped in an Alice in Wonderland world, running faster and faster just to stay in place." Barry Bluestone and Stephen Rose, "Overworked and Underemployed," in *The American Prospect*, March/April 1997, p. 64.

Arlie Russell Hochschild suggests that, among those who do not have to work harder to make ends meet, many nonetheless actually prefer work to home—such is the power of the culture of work over the culture of home and civil society. When people go looking in the workplace for the civic and social values once imparted in the home and neighborhood, the inversion of work and leisure values is complete. See Hochschild, *The Time Bend: When Work Becomes Home and Home Becomes Work* (1997).

9. Don Terry, "Public Housing Program Opens Door to World of Work," *The New York Times*, Jan. 6, 1997.

10. This is the conclusion of Robert Putnam's work on membership in voluntary associations. See Putnam, "Bowling Alone," as well as his "The Strange Disappearance of Civic America," *The American Prospect*, Winter 1996. The many critics who have challenged Putnam for overstating the decline of voluntarism have not separated passive and active forms. Andrew Greeley claims that voluntary service in the United States is higher since 1980, but he also agrees that when the figures are corrected for religion (a primary venue for voluntary activity), the United States loses its lead over other nations. See Andrew Greeley, "The Other Civic America: Religion and Social Capital," *The American Prospect*, May–June

1997. Meanwhile, Sidney Verba and his colleagues note that voluntary activity is badly skewed economically, with the rich volunteering far more than the poor. See Sidney Verba, Kay L. Schlozman, and Henry E. Brady, "The Big Tilt: Participatory Inequality in America," *The American Prospect*, May–June 1997.

11. Frederick Engels, *Socialism: Scientific and Utopian*, in Karl Marx and Frederick Engels, *Selected Works* (Moscow, 1951), II, pp. 140–41.

12. The dream of work is no mere turn of phrase. A recently employed ex-welfare recipient enthused: "I can start deaming again. It feels good to get up every morning and know you have a job to go to." Cited in Don Terry, "Public Housing Program Opens Door to World of Work," *The New York Times*, Jan. 6, 1997.

13. William Greider, *One World, Ready or Not: The Manic Logic of Global Capitalism* (1997), pp. 69–70ff.

14. Judith N. Shklar, *American Citizenship: The Quest for Inclusion* (1991), p. 67.

15. James Carville, *We're Right, They're Wrong!* (1995), p. xvii.

16. See William Julius Wilson, *When Work Disappears: The World of the New Urban Poor* (1996).

17. Joseph Pieper, *Leisure: The Basis of Culture* (1963), p. 19, paraphrasing Plato. This theme, long neglected in the current literature on work and the economy, is fruitfully examined in Sebastian de Grazia's classic work *Time, Work and Leisure* (1962).

18. See Hannah Arendt, *The Human Condition* (1958). Arendt's complex discussion favors the active life over the merely contemplative but roots action in a context of contemplation. In accord with what she recognizes as an "unusual" distinction between the labor of bodies and the work of hands, she also prefers man the maker and creator (*homo faber*) to man the mere laborer, man as animal (*homo laborans*). The modern victory of man the laborer is associated by her with many of the ills of modern life.

19. Rifkin shows persuasively that the service economy—particularly the white-collar service economy of accountants, bankers, lawyers, and brokers, where so many of the "new" jobs are found—is also subject to forces of automation that will give it the same fate as agriculture and the industrial economy. Layoffs and downsizing at information corporations like ATT point the way.

20. Debs cited by Micky Kaus, *The End of Equality* (New York, 1992), p. 136. Carville, *Ibid.*

21. Kaus, p. 140.

22. Rifkin, p. xv.

23. Rifkin offers an illuminating review of such technical solutions but gives little attention to the moral and cultural biases that militate against their success.

24. In *Liberating Feminism* (1976).

25. Beth Belton, "Workers Less Secure," *U.S.A. Today*, Aug. 29, 1997, p. 1.

26. *Ibid.*

27. Cited by Beth Belton, "Workers Less Secure."

28. Restructuring costs of the merger of over a billion dollars are likely to be passed on to the federal government, and thus to the taxpayers. See William Hartung, "Military Monopoly," *The Nation*, Jan. 13/20, 1997.

29. Sebastian de Grazia, *Time, Work and Leisure* (1962). Stanley Parker argues for more public and active forms of leisure in his *The Future of Work and Leisure* (1971), while Joffre Dumazedier promotes the influence that leisure policy can have on securing democracy in his *Towards a Society of Leisure* (1967). See also T. Goodale and G. Godbey, *The Evolution of Leisure* (1988), and Max Kaplan and Phillip Bosserman, eds., *Technology, Human Values, and Leisure* (1971).

30. Low rates of electoral participation, hovering at about 50 percent in American Presidential elections, and descending from higher levels in Europe, are apparent in the analysis of aggregate data. When disaggregated, the data show that the poor, young, and marginalized (people of color in the United States) participate even less. Only one out of five young people between eighteen and twenty-five, for example, vote in elections.

31. This is the true promise of what Harry Boyte calls "public work" in Boyte and Kari, *Building America: The Democratic Promise of Public Work* (1997).

32. See Bruce Ackerman, *The Stakeholder Society* (1998), and Tony Atkinson, *Public Economics at Work* (1997).

33. Lester C. Thurow, in the compendium of op-ed views gathered together in "What's Ahead for Working Men and Women," *The New York Times*, Aug. 31, 1997, p. E9.

34. Just how difficult the task will be is suggested by the skepticism that many theorists express about linking leisure and citizenship. Kenneth Roberts is typical when he writes, "Leisure has not unleashed a flood of effort and commitment into civic organizations . . . participation carries few intrinsic rewards . . . [for] civic participation is not among the most rewarding leisure activities for the mass of people." Robert's conclusion is our challenge: "The growth of leisure has not produced and remains unlikely to produce a new type of participant democracy." Kenneth Roberts, *Contemporary Society and the Growth of Leisure* (1978), pp. 145–46.

INDEX

DATE DUE

		DISCARDED	
			Printed in USA